Wilt Chamberlain: The Inspiring Story of One of Basketball's Greatest Players

An Unauthorized Biography

By: Clayton Geoffreys

Table of Contents

Foreword

Only one player has ever scored 100 points in a single NBA game and that is Wilt Chamberlain. Often considered one of the greatest to ever play the game, Chamberlain dominated the league through the 1960s. He holds several league records including being the only player to average more than forty and fifty points a game in a season. The 1961-1962 season was one for the record books as Wilt averaged 50.4 points a game. It should be no surprise that Chamberlain won the Most Valuable Player award four times over the course of his career and captured two championships in 1967 and 1972. When all was said and done, Wilt would have his jersey retired by the Golden State Warriors, Philadelphia 76ers, and Los Angeles Lakers. Few players have dominated an entire decade of basketball as clearly as Wilt Chamberlain. Thank you for purchasing *Wilt Chamberlain: The Inspiring Story of One of Basketball's Greatest Players*. In this unauthorized biography, we will learn Wilt Chamberlain's incredible life story and impact on the game of basketball. Hope you enjoy and if you do, please do not forget to leave a review!

Also, check out my website at claytongeoffreys.com to join my exclusive list where I let you know about my latest books. To thank you for your purchase, you can go to my site to download a free copy of *33 Life Lessons: Success Principles, Career Advice & Habits of Successful People*. In the book, you'll learn from some of the greatest thought leaders of different industries on what it takes to become successful and how to live a great life.

Cheers,

Clayton Geoffreys

Visit me at www.claytongeoffreys.com

Introduction

Wherever you go, and no matter what culture is concerned, legends, mythologies, and folk tales always say that giants once walked the face of the earth. These giants, as the stories would say, struck terror into the hearts of ordinary folks and were often critical pieces in the establishment of civilizations and numerous cultures and traditions.

While giants are most often confined to the realm of legends and stories, the same cannot be said about the NBA. The NBA has seen its share of giants throughout its long history. These giants have paved the way for the improvement and evolution of the game of basketball. Giants such as Shaquille O'Neal, David Robinson, and Yao Ming are among the most prominent big men the league has ever seen, but they might not have made it into the league if it were not for arguably the NBA's most legendary gigantic figure. That man was Wilt Chamberlain.

Wilt Chamberlain was a giant among men, if there was a term to describe him. Back in the day when the average height of the NBA was merely about 6'5" during the 1960's and when centers were barely 6'10" and power forwards were 6'6", Chamberlain was a towering figure and had earned the nickname "Wilt the Stilt" because of such. But height was not Wilt Chamberlain's best feature.

At 275 lbs. of pure muscle mass, Wilt Chamberlain was a chiseling figure in the middle of the paint. There have been numerous stories about Chamberlain's legendary strength. He used to work out with bodybuilding Arnold Schwarzenegger back in the day and could bench press 500 lbs. He was even so strong that when he blocked a dunk attempt, he dislocated the player's shoulder. And once, when he dunked, the ball went through the basket so hard that it broke the foot of the player that it landed on.[i]

As big and powerful as Wilt Chamberlain was, he was also extremely athletic. Though there was never any official record, stories would say that he had a vertical leap of over 50". This was mainly because he was a high jumper back when he was in high school. In contrast, Michael Jordan had a vertical leap of 48", though he is often considered the league's best high flier in history. Wilt also was not your bumbling and slow giant. In high school, he was a track and field star and could long jump more than 22 feet. If there was an absolute freak of nature in league history, it was Wilt Chamberlain.

As freakishly large, strong, and athletic Wilt Chamberlain was, his basketball feats were just as legendary as any other mythological story in world history. The most famous feat that Wilt had ever done was the 100 points he has scored in a single game back on March 2, 1962, in Hershey, Pennsylvania against the New York Knicks. No other player in league history has ever come close to that performance. The closest to do it was Kobe Bryant when he scored 81 points in 2006. It took more than four decades for a player to break 80 points after Wilt did it. But arguably no player in league history might come close to breaking that 100-point barrier that Chamberlain put up during his playing days. And in contrast, not a lot of teams in today's NBA could even average 100 points in a single game.

Wilt Chamberlain is not only the owner of the highest scoring individual performance of all time, but also has the most rebounds pulled down in a single game. Back on November 24, 1960, Wilt the Stilt recorded an all-time high of 55 rebounds against no less than the Boston Celtics, who had Bill Russell. Russell is considered to be the second best rebounder in league history, and yet Chamberlain was able to effortlessly lord over him inside the paint. The record still stands today as teams would even be hard-pressed to collect 55 rebounds in a single game.

There have been plenty of in-game feats that Wilt Chamberlain put up that have never been duplicated or replicated, and such performances are too many to mention. Along with those feats, Wilt was one of the most accomplished players in league history. Chamberlain was the first player to average more than 30 points a game. He was the first player to win the MVP and the Rookie of Year in the same season. He would earn three more MVP awards to become a four-time winner in that regard. Wilt also led the league in scoring for seven straight seasons and was a rebounding leader for 11 of the 14 seasons he played in the league. And along the way, he even led the league in assists at one point in his career and is the only center to do so in the history of the NBA.

As the most incredible scorer of his time, Chamberlain was once the league's all-time leading scorer. And being the most dominant figure in the history of the league, Wilt the Stilt is the league's all-time leading rebounder with nearly 24,000 career boards collected. But probably the best accomplishments that Wilt Chamberlain ever achieved in his career were the two NBA titles he won as a member of the two different franchises he played for.

Wilt Chamberlain's accomplishments and harrowing feats in the league are almost too impossible to be genuine and are seemingly the stuff you would only hear about in legends. However, they are all true to life facts and achievements that no other player in the long history of the NBA have ever come close to duplicating. Whether one would believe Wilt's legend to be true or not, one can only truly appreciate the mythological NBA giant's feats through the incredible career he forged when the league was still in its early stages.

Chapter 1: Childhood and Early Life

Wilton Norman Chamberlain was born on August 21, 1936, in Philadelphia, Pennsylvania. Before he was the Stilt, Wilt was simply one of nine children born to parents William Chamberlain and Olivia Ruth Johnson. William, the senior Chamberlain, worked as a welder for a publishing company in Philadelphia. He was also a custodian and all-around handyman. Meanwhile, Olivia Ruth was mainly a domestic worker and homemaker.

Though he was already a seemingly tall and large child, Wilt was never fond of basketball. Unlike future giants of the sports like Shaquille O'Neal, who lived and breathed basketball during his childhood, and Yao Ming, who was rumored to be bred to play the game considering both his parents were athletes, six-foot 10-year-old Wilt Chamberlain avoided playing basketball because he thought it was "for sissies."

Instead of paying basketball, Wilt Chamberlain spent his childhood time as a track and field athlete. Seemingly a natural-bred and gifted athlete, the young Chamberlain excelled in that sporting arena. Just how good of a young athlete in track and field was Wilt Chamberlain? Well, he dominated the sport just as he would later become arguably the most dominant player in basketball history.

As a track and field star, Wilt Chamberlain would develop the physical tools he would later use to become a superior athlete compared to his competitors in the NBA. The young Stilt could high jump 6'6" and was pretty quick in the 440 and 880-yard dashes. And as a long jumper, he could jump as far as 22 feet. Even back before he was a basketball superstar, Wilt was already a freak of nature in the most respectful sense of the term.

As he grew older during his teen years, Wilt Chamberlain developed a liking for the sport of basketball. According to him, basketball was the most popular game in Philadelphia. It was in Shoemaker Junior High School when Chamberlain started to play the sport in an organized setting. However, most of his basketball experience during those years was earned in local playgrounds because he had the opportunity to play against older players that were bigger and more physical than the competition he had in junior high.

Chamberlain would start to play more basketball when he entered Overbrook High School. It was then and there when he started his legend as a dominant force of nature mainly because of his height advantage. During his high school years, Wilt the Stilt was already 6'11". Back then, Chamberlain was already a giant of a young man. He was so massive that the kid was already described as a flat-out scary basketball player that changed the game because his peers were not as large as he was.[ii] It was during those high school years when Wilt Chamberlain earned the nickname "The Big Dipper," which was coined because he had to dip his head when passing through doorways.

Chapter 2: High School Career

It was during Wilt Chamberlain's high school years when he became known for his dominant scoring prowess, excellent rebounding abilities, and towering shot-blocking presence inside the paint. He was a one-man wrecking crew for Overbrook High. During his freshman year, the gigantic teenager was already averaging more than 30 points per game and had already led his team to a record of 19-2 that season. Even back then, Chamberlain was unstoppable to the point that opposing players had to double, triple, and quadruple team him so that he could not score the basket. But even so, he averaged 31 points that season and was one win away from winning the city championship.

Wilt Chamberlain was an even more prolific scorer during his sophomore year in Overbrook. One of the most astounding performances he had as a high school player was when he scored 71 points in a win against Roxborough High. Because of his ability to dominate like a man among boys, Chamberlain led the Overbrook Panthers to the Public League championship crown, wherein he top scored with 40 points. He would eventually lead his team to the city title, which had eluded him the last season. Because of him, Overbrook High finished the season undefeated in 19 games.

Before his third season in high school, Wilt Chamberlain had a fond and memorable experience. As a bellboy at Kutsher's Hotel, Chamberlain had the opportunity to meet then-Boston Celtics head coach and legendary basketball figure, Red Auerbach. Auerbach was astonished by the Big Dipper's size and wanted to see how good he was. The legendary head coach would pit Wilt Chamberlain with a Kansas legend named BH Born, who was the NCAA Tournament's Most Outstanding Player in 1953 when his team won the national title. Born was 6'9" and a double-double machine in college.

Red Auerbach told Chamberlain that Born was an All-American and one of the best young players in the country. In essence, the Celtics legend was telling the young Stilt that BH Born would beat him convincingly. However, Born was thoroughly outclassed by the bigger but younger Wilt Chamberlain. He could not score against the more athletic player, who he said could jump and once even hit his head on the rim-holder during that game.[iii]

Chamberlain convincingly won that game 25-10 and led Born to rethink his career path. BH Born had originally planned to play in the NBA to pursue a career as a professional. But after getting outclassed by the high school teenager, he realized that he might not have been good enough for the NBA saying, "if a high school kid was that big and that good, I'd better get a real job." [iii] Because of that, BH Born pursued a career as a tractor engineer but would nevertheless become a major figure in convincing the Big Dipper to play for Kansas University.

In his final year in high school, Wilt Chamberlain was at his best for Overbrook High. The Big Dipper showed his caliber as a future dominant figure in basketball by going for three consecutive games of relentless and unstoppable scoring. In those three games, he topped his 71-point performance the year ago by going for 74, 78, and a ridiculous 90, respectively. In that 90-point game, he scored 60 points in only 12 minutes during the second half of the match. With high-scoring performances such as those, Chamberlain led the Panthers to a third straight Public League title. Then in the City Championship game, Wilt Chamberlain only needed to score 35 points to secure an easy 41-point win over West Catholic.

Wilt Chamberlain ended his final year averaging 44.5 points. He finished high school as Overbrook High's all-time leading scorer and amassed a total of 2,252 points and averaged 37.4 points. Because of how dominant he was as a high school player, there was no need to emphasize that he was the most recruited prep player. Wilt Chamberlain had over 200 college invites after he finished his career at Overbrook.

Wilt Chamberlain was getting recruited by colleges like a king. Varying offers could have persuaded him to join one college program or another. UCLA offered him an opportunity to become a Hollywood actor aside from starring as a basketball phenom. Then, in Philadelphia, the University of Pennsylvania offered him luxurious items such as diamonds just to convince him to stay in the city. However, Wilt Chamberlain shunned the idea of staying in Pennsylvania or anywhere near home because he wanted a change of scenery. As such, playing in New York was also out of the question.

The Midwest was Wilt Chamberlain's only option for college because he did not entertain offers from the Southern states because of how racism and racial segregation was being practiced there. With the sweet talk from former Kansas BH Born and how he loved the school after visiting it, Wilt Chamberlain announced that he was going to attend the University of Kansas to play for head coach Phog Allen.

Chapter 3: College Career

Freshman Year

During those years, freshmen were prohibited from playing for the varsity team of college programs. However, that did not stop Wilt Chamberlain from dominating the game against fellow freshmen to the point that he was getting houses packed full of spectators to see how good he was as a young basketball prodigy.

In December of 1955, the freshmen team had to play against the varsity squad for the annual homecoming game. In the history of the series, the freshman team has never won against the older and more experienced varsity squad. Then came Wilt Chamberlain, the 7-foot giant of a young man. It did not even matter that Chamberlain was playing against a varsity team that had two All-Americans and was a favorite to win the Conference Title.

Showing his legendary stamina, Wilt Chamberlain played the entirety of the game and never rested a single second. He was the biggest target on the floor as his fellow freshmen teammates were looking to set him up inside the paint almost every play. Wilt responded by converting 16 of his 35 field goals to score a game-high 42 points. He had four monstrous two-handed dunks that game and even collected 29 rebounds to add to what was already a terrific performance for the freshman. And for the first time since 1922, the varsity team lost to the freshman year. It was all thanks to Wilt Chamberlain.[iv]

Wilt Chamberlain was so good in that game that his fan following quickly increased. He even impressed a lot of experts so much that they began to call him the greatest basketball player in history at that time. And yes, they were saying that the 19-year-old Wilt Chamberlain was already better than San Francisco collegiate standout Bill Russell and Boston Celtics leading man Bob Cousy. All that was done by a teenager that was yet to make a name for himself in the collegiate ranks.[iv]

Sophomore Season, Varsity Debut Year

After a year of playing for the freshman team, Wilt Chamberlain would finally get a chance to show his dominance as a member of the varsity team. He did not disappoint in his first game. On December 3, 1956, Wilt Chamberlain set two school records in his first official game as a varsity player for Kansas. He scored 52 huge points and had 31 rebounds in a win over Northwestern. In that performance, he broke the all-time Kansas records for points and rebounds.

What Wilt Chamberlain showcased throughout that sophomore year for Kansas was his superhuman stamina and unbelievable endurance. He hardly ever got tired during games and was going full speed the entire 40-minute stretch. He was putting the ball in the basket so fast and getting back on defense so quickly that Chamberlain was the lifeblood of the Kansas Jayhawks.

During the 1957 NCAA Men's Basketball Championship Tournament, Wilt Chamberlain and his team were thoroughly subjected to racial abuse in what was still a segregated city of Dallas. Despite the racial spats, the Kansas Jayhawks led by Wilt the Stilt continued to fight the odds by winning against heavily favored white times.

In the semi-finals of the tournament, Wilt and the Jayhawks had the opportunity to play against San Francisco, which won the last two NCAA championships under the leadership of Bill Russell. Unfortunately, in 1957, Russell had already made his way to the NBA and was unable to meet Chamberlain in the collegiate game for what could have been the first clash between two future rivals. Without Russell, San Francisco could not do anything to stop the Big Dipper. Wilt Chamberlain dominated the two-time defending champions and won by 24 points after going for 32 points, 11 rebounds, and seven blocks.

Wilt Chamberlain was so dominant that he was the leading reason why the Kansas University Jayhawks made it all the way to the national title game against the North Carolina Tar Heels. The Tar Heels' focus the entire night was how to stop or at least stagnate Wilt Chamberlain by making use of what the rules allowed them to do.

In that championship game, North Carolina was playing mind games with the Stilt by making him jump the tip against their shortest player. And in the paint, they sent a bevy of defenders to try to make sure that the big man could not score. A defender was fronting Chamberlain to try to deny him the basket. The secondary man was behind him to defend him in case he got the ball. And when Wilt Chamberlain did indeed catch the ball in the paint, a third defender would come to try to make things harder for the Big Dipper.[ii]

Other than the unorthodox tactics and the triple teams, North Carolina also held onto the ball as long as they could considering that the shot clock was yet to be instituted in the collegiate game at that time. They would instead just pass the ball around to prevent the Jayhawks from getting possession on the other end. However, Kansas fought back until the game went to three overtime periods.[ii] It took until the final play for the Tar Heels to win that bout. With North Carolina leading by a solitary point, Kansas tried to get the ball to the unstoppable Wilt inside the paint. However, the pass was intercepted, and the Tar Heels escaped with the win. Wilt had 23 points and 14 rebounds that night.

Despite losing in that national championship game, Wilt Chamberlain was named the tournament's Most Outstanding Player. He was also named First Team All-American that season after putting up impressive numbers of 29.6 points and 18.9 rebounds for the Kansans Jayhawks. As good as Wilt was in his first season as a varsity player, he was disappointed that it had resulted without a title. That was the first time since high school that Wilt was unable to win a championship despite putting up impressive numbers. He would even, later on, say that the loss to North Carolina was the most painful experience he had as a basketball player.

Junior Year, Final College Season

During the 1957-58 college basketball season, Wilt Chamberlain returned as nation's most dominant player. However, that championship game against the North Carolina Tar Heels paved the way for other teams to stagnate Wilt the Stilt. Throughout that season, opposing teams were triple-teaming and freezing the ball so much that it prevented the Jayhawks from even getting the ball back on the other end just to give the ball to Chamberlain for easy inside baskets.

The games involving the Kansas University Jayhawks were low-scoring and slow because of how opposing teams were freezing possessions and just passing the ball around. Because of this, the Jayhawks players thought that basketball was becoming dull. They were just chasing the ball around while none of their opponents even intended to try to score the basket.

Despite the slower pace and the low amount of possessions, Wilt Chamberlain was still able to average 30.1 points and 17.5 rebounds the entire season. He was also named First Team All-American that season. However, the Kansans Jayhawks were unable to secure the conference title and only finished second. At that time, only conference winners were allowed to play in the NCAA Tournament. Because of that, the Jayhawks missed the chance to play for the national championships.

Despite missing the NCAA Tournament, Wilt the Stilt was excelling in other fields. Proving how incredible of an athlete and how superhuman his body was, Wilt Chamberlain was also a track and field star for Kansas, though he was already playing intense basketball on a regular basis for the Jayhawks. Chamberlain was so fast and athletic that he could run 100 yards in 10.9 seconds. His triple jump showcased his insanely inhuman leaping ability after he recorded 50 feet in that department. And in the three years he spent with Kansas, he was unbeatable in the Big 8 high jump competition. That just goes to show how great of an athlete Wilt Chamberlain was.

However, by the end of the season, Wilt Chamberlain decided that he had already lost interest in the college game and was instead inclined towards using his talents to earn money. He already wanted to play professional basketball after choosing to forego his senior year in college. In the two seasons he played varsity basketball for the Kansas Jayhawks, Wilt the Stilt averaged 29.9 points and 18.3 rebounds.

Back in the day, a player's recruitment class must first graduate from college before he can make himself eligible for the NBA. Because Wilt Chamberlain's class still had one more year left, the Big Dipper had to wait one more season before he could try his hand at the big leagues. Because of that, Wilt Chamberlain decided instead to go professional by playing for the Harlem Globetrotters instead.

Chapter 4: Harlem Globetrotters Career

Because of the eligibility rules that hindered him from going straight to the NBA, Wilt Chamberlain had to look elsewhere. He would decide to play for the Harlem Globetrotters in the one year that he needed to wait for before his recruitment class would graduate from college. He signed a $50,000 contract with the Globetrotters for the one year he would play for that team. In contrast, most NBA players that time were only making $9,000.

Despite being a professional basketball team, the Harlem Globetrotters were more of an exhibition squad rather than one that played competitively. The Globetrotters would play against several other teams that acted as stooges for them while they were entertaining crowds with exhibition plays that were combinations of athletic display, comedy, showboating, and even theater. They would tour around the country, and even the world doing exhibition shows to wow audiences and show a brighter side of basketball.

Wilt Chamberlain was a member of the Globetrotter team that made history by making it all the way to the former USSR to play a game in Moscow. The Soviet crowd openly welcomed the American basketball artists while the USA and USSR relationship was steadily improving. The show was sold out in Moscow, and this was also due in part to how Chamberlain was quickly becoming a household name in international basketball despite not even playing a single game of competitive professional basketball.

As a display of Wilt Chamberlain's freakish strength, one of the skits that the Globetrotters involved the legendary Meadowlark Lemon falling to the ground and the Big Dipper helping him up. But Wilt the Stilt would not just help him up the conventional way. Instead, Chamberlain would pick him up from the ground and toss him up like a rag doll only to catch him mid-air. This was not a simple feat considering that Meadowlark Lemon was at least 6'2" and weighed north of 200 pounds. This led to Lemon himself saying that Wilt Chamberlain was the strongest basketball player he has ever encountered in his life.

Wilt Chamberlain would spend only one year with the Harlem Globetrotters and would immediately make his name in the NBA the following year despite the fact that he hardly played competitive basketball during the time he spent waiting for his class to graduate from college.

Chapter 5: NBA Career

Territorial Pick

One of the rules in effect in the NBA since 1955 up to that point in time was the territorial draft. The draft allowed an NBA team to give up its conventional first round draft pick in exchange for the rights to claim a local college player. The purpose of the territorial draft was to allow the team to make use of the following that the college player had developed in that area over the four years he had played there.

Back when Wilt was in high school, Red Auerbach even tried to convince the young basketball stud to play for New England in Boston so that the Celtics could claim him as their territorial pick. But history would show that Chamberlain decided to play elsewhere. Instead, the Celtics landed an equally great player in Bill Russell, who would later form a legendary duo with Wilt Chamberlain, who was still then trying to make his way to the NBA.

The problem, however, was that Wilt Chamberlain played his college basketball at Kansas, which had no NBA team at that time. The Warriors, who were based in Chamberlain's home city of Philadelphia at that time, were trying to claim Chamberlain as their territorial pick on the argument that the Big Dipper had spent his entire pre-college years in their city and that Kansas had no NBA team that could claim the big young man. The league would agree with that argument and would allow the Philadelphia Warriors to claim Wilt Chamberlain, who was already a familiar household name in the city he grew up in.[v]

There was a good reason for the Philadelphia Warriors to give up their first round draft choice just to pick Wilt Chamberlain as their territorial draftee instead. It was even a no-brainer that Wilt the Stilt was going to be the most dominant rookie in his graduating class and was arguably even going to be one of the top players in the league the moment he entered the NBA.

Before he was a pro, Wilt Chamberlain was a skinny 7-footer that weighed about 225 pounds during his freshman year in college. However, he gradually gained muscle mass and eventually became arguably the strongest basketball player of his time. And while standing barefooted, the goliath of a young man could reach 9'6" with his arms straight up. He was not only tall but was also unbelievably long. With that, Chamberlain was already a towering and unstoppable physical presence during his college years.

During his early years as a basketball player, what Wilt Chamberlain used to dominate the game of basketball was his superior athletic abilities that nobody else in the league has been able to match. Despite his height and frame, Wilt the Stilt could move as agile as any point guard in the league thanks to his background in track and field. As a leaper, Wilt could jump higher than any other basketball player in the world and was a three-time high jump champion in the Big 8 Conference in college. He could even triple jump over 50 feet when he was still with Kansas. With all those physical and athletic tools, there was no wonder that the Big Dipper was seemingly a man among boys whenever he played basketball.

As his college seasons went by, Wilt Chamberlain learned not to rely on his physical gifts only. He developed an array of uncanny moves inside the paint, though he could already get by with his size, height, and length. One of Wilt Chamberlain's earliest go-to moves was a right-handed shot he could pull off by faking his shoulder from left to right. And whenever he was far away from the basket, the Big Dipper would use his superior speed to drive past his defenders down the middle of the lane and then use his go-to shoulder fake to get position inside the basket for a right-handed shot or a monstrous dunk. Other than that, he also knew how to bank his shots in whenever he was not in the position to drive or score inside.[iv]

By the time Wilt Chamberlain was a force to be reckoned with in the college ranks, he already had an unstoppable array of offensive moves to complement his already inhuman athletic capabilities. Wilt was not only confined to doing his shoulder fake moves and bank shots but had also developed a consistent jump hook inside the lane. He would often even go for turnaround jumpers over smaller defenders. But nothing, other than his monstrous dunks, defined his offense more than his silky finger rolls close to the basket. Chamberlain was not only a freakish athlete but was also already a smooth operator inside the paint.

What made Wilt Chamberlain so good was not his physical stature or his offensive moves. It was his superhuman stamina that made him a rare specimen. With his track and field background, Chamberlain can go through fast-paced games without sitting on the bench for a few seconds. He would play most of his games from the first tip until the final buzzer to signal the end of the bout. And during the entire game, he would play intensely without looking winded. His stamina allowed him to stay in the match long enough to produce eye-popping stats that nobody had ever seen in the NBA.

If there were any weaknesses in Wilt Chamberlain's offensive game, it was that he did not have the most reliable jump shot. Spending most of his basketball years dominating under and close to the basket over defenders he would tower over, the Big Dipper never had to settle for jump shots several feet away from the goal. When players during that era were more fundamentally sound in the sense that their offensive arsenals were more or less complete, Chamberlain was missing the jump shot that would have made him an even more unstoppable scoring machine.

On the defensive end, Wilt Chamberlain was not the same defensive presence as two-time NCAA champion Bill Russell was. Russell relied more on his ability to protect the basket, not only by blocking shots, but by contesting the opposing team's scoring opportunities. He made his name as a defender while Chamberlain was more of an offensive force. Despite that, Wilt had a knack for blocking shots all the way out to the bleachers. He was a tremendous shot blocker but did not contest shots he thought he could not block. It was described that Wilt was the kind of player that was not so aggressive on the defensive end and did not raise his freakishly long arms enough to be able to bother shots he could not block.[iv]

Other than that, Wilt Chamberlain was as complete of a center as any other player in league history. He was an anomaly in the annals of not only the NBA, but also the entire sport. And as good as he was in Kansas and as entertainingly athletic as he was with the Harlem Globetrotters, his ultimate fate would be decided once he stepped on an NBA court for an official game. Whether he would be just as dominant in the professional league was up for him and the NBA to decide.

Rookie Season, the Rookie MVP

Before the Philadelphia Warriors drafted Wilt Chamberlain, they were a mediocre team that had to rely on two-time scoring leader Paul Arizin to do the heavy lifting. However, not even the legendary player was able to lift the Warriors out of the hump. And while Paul Arizin might have been the alpha male of the Warriors in prior seasons, it became apparent that it had already become Wilt Chamberlain's team the moment the Stilt slipped on his Philadelphia jersey on.

In only his first game as an NBA player, Wilt Chamberlain had already made it known that he was out to take the league by storm. In his NBA debut on October 24, 1959, Chamberlain put up 43 points on a 17 out of 27 shooting clip from the field. He would also collect 28 rebounds after playing almost the entire 48-minute length of that win against the New York Knicks. Then, in his second game, Wilt put up 36 points and 34 rebounds for his first ever 30-30 game in that win over the Detroit Pistons. He would immediately top that on November 4 after going for the first ever 40-40 game. Chamberlain finished that win against the Syracuse Nationals with 41 points and 40 rebounds.

On November 7, Wilt Chamberlain would meet Bill Russell for the first time in what was to become one of the earliest known basketball rivalries in NBA history. Chamberlain was quickly becoming known as an offensive and rebounding juggernaut. Meanwhile, Russell had already established himself as the premier defensive presence in the NBA. The two early-era giants squared off as both Wilt and Bill played the entire game. That first battle was a showcase of how different the two players were. The Stilt put up as many shots as he could to score as many points as possible. Meanwhile, Russell controlled the rebounds and held his own against the mammoth of a man known as the Big Dipper.

In the end, it was a stalemate. Wilt the Stilt finished with 30 points and 28 rebounds. However, Russell's defense frustrated the young monster, who only shot 12 out of 38 from the field in that game. In contrast, Bill Russell finished with 22 points and 35 rebounds. It also showed how different the two giants were. Chamberlain was garnering attention with his monstrous stats. Meanwhile, Bill Russell, who led the Celtics to a win that night, was regarded as the better leader and winner between the two legends.

After that loss to the Celtics, the Warriors would end up winning five of their next six games to start the season 8-2. In one of those six games, Wilt put up his first ever career 50-point game. In what was then regarded as his career high, which he would later break over and over again, Chamberlain scored 55 points in addition to the 29 rebounds he had in a win against the Cincinnati Royals on November 12. Overall in only his first ten games as an NBA star, the Big Dipper averaged 37.1 points and 31.5 rebounds.

As the season went by, it became apparent that Wilt Chamberlain was becoming basketball's most dominant player of all time. He was even regarded as the best player in league history as a rookie that season. Chamberlain's 40-point games and 30-rebound performances quickly became a norm for him and the crowd, and the giant was not showing signs of slowing down.

Considering that the NBA only had eight teams that time, it was unavoidable that Wilt Chamberlain would have to face Bill Russell several times. Late in November, he won back-to-back meetings against Russell's Celtics and put up monstrous numbers in both those bouts. In the first win on November 25, he had 45 points and 35 rebounds. The next night, he had 49 points and 33 rebounds. But not even Wilt the Stilt was unstoppable, and Russell would shut him in their next two meetings, which were both losses for the Philadelphia Warriors. And even after putting up his second 40-40 game on January 15, 1960, Chamberlain's 44 points and 43 rebounds were not enough to get a win against Russell, who was already up four wins to three against his eternal rival at that point.

Wilt Chamberlain would be named an All-Star for the very first time in his career. On that January 22 night, he was even the star among stars though he was playing with and against the best of the best in the NBA. In leading the Eastern Conference team to a win, Wilt the Stilt was named the All-Star MVP after going for 23 points and 25 rebounds.

On January 25, Wilt Chamberlain went for a new career high and his second career 50-point game. Against the Detroit Pistons, he was an unstoppable wrecking ball that demolished defenders in the paint. Wilt converted 24 of his 41 field goals to score 58 points. He also collected 42 rebounds to finish with his third career game of scoring 40 points and collecting 40 rebounds. That was also the NBA's first 50-40 game.

Wilt Chamberlain would tie his career mark on February 21 against the New York Knicks. In that match, he made 26 out of 47 of his field goals to score a total of 58 points. He also added 24 rebounds for good measure in that win over the Knicks. And two nights later in a game against the Boston Celtics, he scored at least 50 points for the fourth time that season after leading his team to a win. He had 53 points and 29 rebounds in what was another clash between the two biggest names in the NBA.

By the end of the season, Wilt Chamberlain had broken several of the NBA's records. His point-rebound average also effectively broke the record for points per game and rebounds per game in a single season. Chamberlain averaged 37.6 points, which was the very first time in league history that a player scored over 30 in a single season. His 27-rebound average was also a league record at that point. Impressively, Wilt the Stilt also broke what was then regarded as the best scoring season of any player. During the past season, Bob Pettit averaged over 29 points and amassed a total of more than 2100 points in a span of 72 games. Meanwhile, the Big Dipper only needed 56 games to reach the 2100-point mark and had a total of over 2,700 during that season.

With the way Wilt Chamberlain captivated the crowd and dominated the league as a newcomer, the Stilt was named the league's Most Valuable Player. Of course, he was also awarded the Rookie of the Year trophy to become the first player to win that award along with the MVP in the same season. Only Wes Unseld in later years was able to duplicate such a feat. But as dominant as Wilt was in his rookie season after breaking records and amassing awards after awards, the only thing he needed to win was the NBA title to cap off what is arguably the best season by a newcomer.

In the playoffs, the Philadelphia Warriors were set to square off against the Syracuse Nationals in a best-of-three series in the Division Semi-finals. Chamberlain opened that series by going for 35 points and 27 rebounds in what was a 23-point win for the Warriors in that first game. The Nationals would bounce back in Game 2, but Wilt thoroughly outclassed their entire roster in Game 3. In that clinching game, the Big Dipper finished with a then-career playoff high of 53 points to go along with 22 rebounds to secure a date against the Boston Celtics in the Division Finals.

While Wilt Chamberlain and Bill Russell have both faced each other numerous times during the regular season and have probably already familiarized each other's tendencies, the playoffs were an entirely different playing field. Fighting for a chance at a title meant more physicality and intensity. The same was true for the two Goliaths squaring off in the proverbial gladiatorial ring known as the basketball court.

In Game 1 of that best-of-seven series, Wilt the Stilt made it known that he was out for blood. He finished that game with 42 points and 29 rebounds. Unfortunately, Red Auerbach had a plan to neutralize the giant, not on the scoring end of the floor, but the defensive side of the game. The Celtics conceded to the fact that Wilt was an unstoppable scorer. Instead, they controlled his ability to defend the basket by shoving him and playing him physically before he could run back to the Warriors' defensive end of the floor to contest shots. With Chamberlain struggling to get back on defense, the Celtics could easily score fastbreak points without a prolific shot blocker protecting the basket. While the Celtics employed the same strategy in Game 2, the Warriors ended up winning it to tie the series one win apiece.

In Game 3, however, the Boston Celtics were clicking on all cylinders on the offensive end while containing Chamberlain on their defensive end to take the bout by 30 points. In that game, Wilt the Stilt looked mortal. For only the second time in his career at that point, the Big Dipper scored below 20 points after tallying only 12 markers in that blowout loss. The first time he was limited to below 20 points was when he only played 9 minutes on February 10 in a loss to the New York Knicks. And while the Stilt was marginally better in Game 4, the Celtics still ended up winning that matchup to go up 3-1.

Not willing to cede the title opportunity to the Boston Celtics, Wilt Chamberlain went on a rampage in what was a blowout win for the Philadelphia Warriors in Game 5. Chamberlain scored 22 of his 42 field goals to finish the game with 50 points and 35 rebounds. This, in turn, forced Game 6, which was still a do-or-die moment for Wilt and his Warriors.

Both Chamberlain and Russell neutralized one another in Game 6. Wilt was trying to get to his first NBA Finals to cap off what was already the best rookie season in league history. Meanwhile, Bill was gunning for his third championship ring after already winning two of them. The giants were shoving and getting physical with one another inside the paint for a chance at an NBA title. The Stilt finished that game with 26 points and 24 rebounds. His rival had a similar stat line of 25 points and 25 rebounds.

With the two mammoths fighting to a stalemate, it boiled down to their backups to try to win the game for them. As it was always true throughout the rivalry between Chamberlain and Russell, the latter always had a better supporting cast and coach. Unlike Wilt, Bill was not a one-man wrecking crew and had other All-Star players that eased the burden off of him. Because of that, the Celtics won Game 6 and would eventually take the NBA title in seven games against the St. Louis Hawks in the Finals.

Despite bowing out of the playoffs in the Division Finals and finishing the season without a title, there was no argument that Wilt Chamberlain's rookie year was the best in the history of the NBA. He was the MVP and the Rookie of the Year at the same time while breaking numerous scoring and rebounding records in the process despite his relative lack of experience. And as good as Wilt the Stilt was during his rookie year, it was only a prelude of what was to come.

Continued Dominance

After that historic rookie season, Wilt Chamberlain surprised fans and basketball followers alike when he said that he was contemplating retiring from the game of basketball after only one year. The reason for that was that he was tired of how defenses were treating him. He was getting doubled and tripled every single game while defenders were not exactly trying to go soft on him. The Stilt was taking the type of physical beating that no other player up to that point had gotten, and Wilt feared the day that he might retaliate against all the pounding he was getting. He also did not like the rough treatment he was getting from opposing fans. Chamberlain was often ridiculed because of his size, and that did not sit well with him.[v]

Chamberlain did not retire after then-Warriors owner Eddie Gottlieb raised his salary to a record of $65,000 annually. Instead of always enduring the brunt of the physical plays against him, the Big Dipper retaliated by making sure he would not feel the pain of the hard fouls he was getting. Wilt Chamberlain spent the offseason bulking up and becoming stronger than ever. He did that every year to make sure that he was in the best physical shape to take the pounding that mortal players could not. From 225 pounds during his freshman season in Kansas, he bulked up to an average of 275 pounds of lean muscle mass during his NBA career. He even reached as heavy as 300 pounds later in his career.[vi]

Wilt Chamberlain opened his second season in the league going for 42 points and 31 rebounds in a win against the Syracuse Nationals on October 22, 1960. After putting up at least 20 points and 20 rebounds in the next three games, he would explode for 44 points and 39 rebounds against the Detroit Pistons on November 4 in a win for the Philadelphia Warriors, who were then still undefeated in five games.

With Wilt the Stilt leading them, the Warriors would eventually start their season winning nine games in a row. During that span, Chamberlain averaged 34.6 points and 29 rebounds for the Philadelphia Warriors, who were still leaning on their Big Dipper for the points and rebounds they needed to win games. It was a two-point loss to the St. Louis Hawks on November 12 that snapped the Warriors' 9-0 start. Wilt had 42 points and 24 rebounds that night.

It was on November 24 of that year when Wilt Chamberlain went for the first of his many unbreakable records. In a bout against no less than the Boston Celtics and Bill Russell, the Big Dipper was a vacuum cleaner on the boards. With the Celtics and Russell defending him extremely well, Chamberlain missed 27 of the 42 field goals he attempted. His team, which shot barely 41% that night, did not do well on the scoring end, either. This only meant that there were more offensive rebounding opportunities for him.

Wilt Chamberlain was gobbling up every rebound to give more possessions to his team that night. Nobody could stop him from grabbing every missed shot. Not even Bill Russell, regarded as the second greatest rebounder ever and the only player close enough to Chamberlain's rebounding numbers, could contain the Stilt. Wilt Chamberlain would eventually grab a total of 55 rebounds that night while trying to give his team the win. Sadly, the Warriors could not win that game despite the historic performance that Chamberlain had. In contrast, the Celtics only had 59 rebounds that night. Wilt was only five rebounds shy of outrebounding an entire team.

That 55-rebound night remains one of the NBA's untouchable and unbreakable records to this day. Wilt has owned almost every top rebounding game the league has ever seen. And since 1973 when the league started counting offensive rebounds and the NBA was slowly modernizing into what it is right now, the highest rebounding game was Moses Malone's 37-rebound night in February 1979. During the 80's, the highest rebounding performance was when Charles Oakley collected 35 boards. During the 90's, Dennis Rodman had a decade-high of 32 rebounds. And in the modern era, Kevin Love collected 31 rebounds back in 2010. No player has ever come close to breaking that record that 55-rebound performance.

Today, not even a lot of teams can even collect 55 rebounds in a game. During the 2016-17 season, the highest rebound per game average by any team was a little under 47 boards a night. While eras may be different and Wilt's generation played a faster pace, it only goes to show that it is already seemingly impossible to break that 55-rebound performance considering that today's NBA teams would even struggle to collect 50 rebounds in a single night. What more could one modern-era player do if his team could not even break Chamberlain's record? We may never see a player that could break that record. Wilt's name as the league's best rebounder could eternally stay on top of the list.

Throughout the season, Wilt Chamberlain consistently scored over 40 points and collected nearly 30 rebounds a night. And that season, he also scored at least 50 points more than he did back when he was a rookie. The first time Wilt did so was on January 2, 1961, against the New York Knicks. Chamberlain finished that game with 56 points after making 23 of his 37 shots. He also added 28 rebounds to his name that night.

Wilt the Stilt replicated that performance three nights later. Against the Syracuse Nationals in a win, Chamberlain had 56 points on 20 out of 32 shooting from the floor in addition to the 26 rebounds he gobbled up that evening. That game was the fourth bout of Wilt Chamberlain's four-game streak of scoring at least 46 points. He averaged 52 points and 28 rebounds during those four games.

On January 21, Chamberlain would again score 56 points against the Los Angeles Lakers. Draining 25 of his 46 shots, Wilt had 56 points and also added 45 rebounds for another career 50-40 game. The fourth time he would score at least 50 that season was on February 3 against the Cincinnati Royals. He had 52 that night. And in the next game, he had 55 points and 29 rebounds in an overtime win against the New York Knicks.

Wilt Chamberlain would tie his career high in points on February 25 of that year. In that win against the Royals, the Big Dipper finished with 58 points on a 25 out of 38 shooting clip. And barely a week later, he would score 56 points for the fourth time that season when the Warriors lost to the Nationals despite the tremendous effort from their main gun.

On March 9, 1961, Wilt Chamberlain recorded a new career high in points as well as the second highest scoring individual game by any player at that time in the history of the league. Against the Knicks in a win that night, Chamberlain could not miss. He drained 27 of his 37 field goal attempts to score 67 points. He also collected 31 rebounds in the process. That performance was second only to the 71 points that Elgin Baylor scored back in November 1960 of that same season. At that juncture of NBA history, Wilt's 67-point performance was the second highest scoring performance by any player, but he would rewrite that over and over again as his career progressed.

By the end of the season, Wilt Chamberlain increased his averages to 38.4 points and 27.2 rebounds. He once again rewrote history by averaging the most points and rebounds ever up to that point. His 27.2-rebounding average that season still stands as the best in that regard in league history. Wilt Chamberlain also became the first and only player have at least 3,000 points and 2,000 rebounds in the same season. Wilt was the first ever player to score 3,000 points in a single season. Michael Jordan is the only other player to have ever reached that mark after Chamberlain did it in 1961 and over and over again during his entire career. And nobody other than the Big Dipper has ever collected at least 2,000 rebounds in one season. Although he was still regarded the best and most dominant player in NBA history, he would lose the MVP award to Bill Russell after the Celtics great led his team to a much better season than what Chamberlain had with the Philadelphia Warriors.

An NBA Championship would have been the perfect prize for Wilt Chamberlain that season to secure his place as arguably the best to have ever played the game of basketball. However, he did not even come close to that. Sporting the same supporting cast he had when the Warriors lost to the Celtics the prior year, Chamberlain could not do enough to even win a single game against the Syracuse Nationals in the Division Semi-finals of the playoffs. It was an early exit for Wilt Chamberlain and his Philadelphia Warriors.

The Historic Scoring Season, the 100-Point Game

Frank McGuire, the coach responsible for leading the North Carolina Tar Heels against Wilt Chamberlain's Kansas University Jayhawks back in the 1957 NCAA Finals, would replace former head coach Neil Johnston because the latter was unable to see eye-to-eye with the Big Dipper in the figurative sense. Owner Frank Gottlieb believed that McGuire was strong-willed enough to know how to handle Chamberlain's difficult personality and how to unleash the monstrous capabilities of the already unstoppable scoring and rebounding machine. With McGuire as the head coach, the Stilt became an unstoppable force of nature that scored at will and destroyed opponents with ease.

In the first five games of the Philadelphia Warriors, Wilt Chamberlain could not be contained. He started the season out with 48 points and 25 rebounds in a loss to the Lakers on October 19, 1961. He followed that up with 57 points and 32 rebounds against the very same team the following day. Then, against the Knicks on October 21, Chamberlain delivered 53 points and 35 rebounds before going for 55 points against the Syracuse Nationals six days later. Wilt would round out that five-game scoring barrage on October 28 by going for 43 points and 23 boards versus the Nationals in a win. In those five games, Wilt Chamberlain averaged 51.2 points and 28 rebounds. While it was relatively easy for Wilt to average at least 50 points in short stretches during that season, nobody expected him to do so the entire campaign.

On November 4, Wilt Chamberlain resumed his scoring dominance by going for three straight games of scoring at least 55 points. He had back-to-back 58-point games against the Detroit Pistons in consecutive meetings against them before going for 55 points on November 9 against the Nationals in a 43-point blowout victory. But Wilt the Stilt was not done yet.

Against the Los Angeles Lakers on December 1, Wilt Chamberlain scored at least 60 points for the second time in his career after delivering 60 markers in a win. When everybody thought that Wilt was done, he was only getting started. A week later against the very same Laker team, he rewrote history by turning in a new career high and a new single-game NBA record for points scored by a player. Though it came in a loss, Wilt drained half of his 62 field goals to score 78 points in triple-overtime. As a testament to his ironman stamina, Chamberlain played all 63 minutes of that game. He also collected 43 rebounds to turn in what was the first 70-40 game in league history.

As an encore of sorts, Wilt Chamberlain would have 61 points and 36 rebounds the following day in a win against the new Chicago Packers team to show that not even 63 minutes the prior night could gas him out. Chamberlain would score at least 50 points ten more times in December after that 78-point performance. He scored 60 points one more time that month when he put up 60 and 26 against the Lakers again on December 29. During December of 1961, the Big Dipper averaged godlike numbers of 52.4 points and 26.1 rebounds.

On January 13, 1962, Wilt Chamberlain would have his second career 70-point game after going for 73 points on 29 out of 48 shooting in a win against the Packers. Because of that performance, Wilt Chamberlain became the owner of the two highest scoring single-game performances in league history. He also added 36 rebounds to his name in that win. Wilt the Stilt would then score 62 points in each of the next two games to show that he was not slowing down anytime soon after turning in back-to-back high-scoring outputs. He would have 62 points one more time that month in an overtime win against Syracuse on January 21. Wilt averaged 52 points and 25 rebounds during that month.

Late in February, Wilt Chamberlain would start what is arguably the greatest five-game scoring stretch in league history. He started off with 67 points on 25 out of 38 shooting from the floor against the Knicks on February 25 before scoring 65 points and collecting 23 rebounds versus the St. Louis Hawks on February 27. A night after that, he would go for 61 markers against Chicago. He would end that five-game run with 58 points against the Knicks on March 4, but that was not the icing on the cake.

On the historic day of March 2, 1962, Wilt Chamberlain and the Philadelphia Warriors would welcome the New York Knicks to Hershey, Pennsylvania, but nobody in attendance expected what they were about to see. Just after scoring three straight 60-point performances, Chamberlain was not yet done or exhausted yet. He wanted more.

Wilt Chamberlain dominated the New York Knicks' centers throughout that night after scoring 23 points in the first quarter alone. He would go on to finish the first half with 41 points as it became apparent that the Big Dipper was primed for something special that evening. He would then score 28 more points to total 69 markers by the end of the third quarter as the crowd began to chant "Give it to Wilt!" knowing that they were about to see history unfolding before their eyes.[vii]

The team responded because they also wanted their center to do the unthinkable and seemingly impossible. Not wanting Chamberlain to abuse and embarrass them, the New York Knicks fouled all the other Warriors to prevent them from handing the ball to the gigantic man in the middle. Countering such a tactic, the Philadelphia Warriors would in turn foul a Knick over at the other end to make sure that they would have more possessions and that Wilt would have more chances to score the ball.[vii] The game was already decided, but all the crowd wanted to see was for the Big Dipper to go for a historic record.

When the game was nearing its end, Wilt Chamberlain caught a pass and went straight up for a close-range shot that went in. That shot was the one that gave him a tally of 100 total points scored that night. Knowing he had just made history, the Stilt ran back over to the other end and straight to the locker room as the game was decided in favor of the Philadelphia Warriors.

It was during that locker room moment when the public relations representative Harvey Pollack went for a piece of paper and wrote "100" on it. He gave it to Wilt, who then had pictures taken with him showing off that paper. That photo of Wilt Chamberlain holding up that piece of paper remains to be the most iconic photo in all of basketball history because no other player before or after him has ever done what he had just accomplished that night.

By scoring 100 points on 36 out of 63 shooting from the field and on 28 out of 32 shooting from the free throw line, Wilt Chamberlain outscored and outdone his previous high of 78 points. He became the owner of the three highest scoring single-game performances in league history after that performance. His accomplishment on that night of March 2, 1962, remains one of the best moments in league history and still stands as the highest scoring game ever. No other player has come close to breaking his 100-point output.

The only other player to have ever had the best chance of coming close to that performance was Kobe Bryant. Fast forward to January 22, 2006 (more than four decades later), Bryant scored 81 points against the Toronto Raptors to own the second highest single-game scoring record by any player in league history. Despite that performance, he was still 19 points shy of Chamberlain's record.

Some would argue that Bryant's performance was better than Wilt's 100-point game. Back in 1962, the pace was a lot faster, and teams had more opportunities to score. In 2006, the game slowed down a bit and defenses as well as the talents and athletic capabilities of the players were far superior to what they were in 1962. And given that Kobe was more of a perimeter player, the fact that he was draining jumper after jumper was considered more impressive than Wilt Chamberlain, who was dunking and shooting over smaller defenders within five feet away from the basket.

However, there would still be some that would argue that Wilt Chamberlain's 100-point game is still far more impressive than what Kobe Bryant did in 2006. Back in Chamberlain's day, there was no three-point line whereas the three-point shot was one of the weapons that Kobe used to score 81 points. While Wilt was not expected to shoot 25 feet away from the basket assuming that the three-point line had been instituted in 1962, it would have been easier for him to score baskets inside the paint.

Because the three-point line is the most potent weapon in today's NBA, teams stretch their defenses out to the perimeter and open the paint up for potential attacks by big men. Back in Wilt's day when there was still no three-point line, teams would pack their defenses close to the basket because there was no incentive for them to guard beyond 20 feet away because all shots were counted as two points no matter the distance. Because of that, Wilt was probably taking the brunt of multiple defenders crowding on him during that 100-point performance. Had there been a three-point line, defenders would have been reluctant to focus on him inside the paint because of the presence of shooters roaming outside the perimeter.

And what also makes Wilt Chamberlain's 100-point performance more impressive than Bryant's 81-point output was the fact that he had better teammates as far as production went. The Warriors had productive players in the likes of Paul Arizin, Guy Rodgers, and Tom Gola that season. Those players are capable of scoring 20 points or more on any given night, but the Big Dipper was the one that owned the box score on March 2, 1962. In comparison, Kobe's best teammate in 2006 was Lamar Odom, who never became an All-Star. Because of that, it was understandable for Bryant to hog all the shot attempts.

Taking nothing away from Kobe Bryant's performance, there is still no arguing that Wilt Chamberlain's 100-point game is still the best single-game performance in league history. Although those 100 points seem too much for any player to score in today's modern game, the evolution of today's NBA has made it more possible for players to come close to what Wilt has achieved during his time.

Today's modern NBA has returned to its fast-paced style, though it still is not on par with the pace played back in the 1960's. But the great equalizer that today's era has is the three-point shot, which has grown to become the most potent weapon in the league. The three-pointer has been used more than it has ever been since its inception and could be the reason why a player could someday come near or even crack Chamberlain's record. Most of today's best scorers are phenomenal three-point shooters. You have Kevin Durant, Steph Curry, James Harden, and Russell Westbrook, who are all capable of scoring in bunches and draining long jumpers from a distance. But while it does not seem impossible for any player to break Wilt's record, the fact of the matter is that no active player today has come close to doing so. We might one day see a transcendent scorer breaking Chamberlain's record, but as of today, it seems like a distant prospect.

Returning to 1962, Wilt Chamberlain finished the regular season averaging new and still standing NBA record of 50.4 points in an entire season. Before Chamberlain, no player has averaged even 30 points a game during the regular season. But Wilt even skipped averaging at least 40 points to norm 50 during the 1961-62 season. He rewrote history books by adding 12 points to the 38.4 points he averaged a year ago. No player has ever come close to averaging 50 points or even averaged 40 a game. Only Wilt Chamberlain has done it, and that was how dominant he was the entire season.

In addition to the 50.4 points he averaged that season, Chamberlain also averaged an NBA record of 48.4 minutes a night. While NBA games are only 48 minutes long, Wilt surpassed that because of the overtime periods he played that season. Playing entire games that season, Wilt was the personification of stamina. He never got too fatigued and would still go at it every single night despite playing the full length of an NBA game. This was yet another one of Wilt Chamberlain's superhuman accomplishments.

Compared to today's era, not a lot of centers would even average more than 40 minutes a night despite the fact that games are played slower, defenses are less physical due to the new rules, and medical treatment has made it more possible for players to come into games healthier. In Chamberlain's case, he had to play in an era where the pace was faster, the rules were lenient, and the advancements in health and sports sciences were light years away from what they are today. Was Wilt Chamberlain an android because of his stamina? Well, he certainly was human, but he could have been superhuman from the looks of it.

In addition to the scoring records he set that season, Wilt Chamberlain also set a then All-Star Game scoring record of 42 points though the East lost that game against the West. It would take five and a half decades for someone to break that record. Anthony Davis would score

52 points in the 2017 All-Star Game to break the 55-year record that Wilt Chamberlain held.

Despite Wilt Chamberlain's historic and record-setting season, he was not named the league MVP. Even Oscar Robertson, who averaged a triple-double for the first and only time up to that point in league history, was not the MVP. The award was given to Bill Russell yet again because of how he dominated the leadership role of the seemingly unbeatable Boston Celtics. Throughout Wilt's career, Russell was the biggest thorn that he found most difficult to pluck out.

During that year, the Division Semis were changed from a three-game series to a best-of-five contest to determine who proceeded to the Division Finals. For the third straight year, the Philadelphia Warriors faced the Syracuse Nationals, who they beat two seasons ago but failed to defend against during the last playoffs. That 1962 series between the Warriors and the Nationals was the tiebreaker.

Wilt Chamberlain did not waste time in trying to force his team to the next round. He scored 32 points and collected 25 rebounds in Game 1 to draw first blood against the Nationals. Then, in Game 2, he would go for 28 points and 26 rebounds for a comfortable win as the Philadelphia Warriors improved their lead to 2-0 against a seemingly helpless Syracuse team. However, the Nationals bounced back to win the next two games in close fashion and forced a deciding fifth game. In that final game of the series, there was no nonsense in Wilt Chamberlain's eyes. The greatest player in basketball took it upon himself to beat the Nationals almost singlehandedly. He scored a new career playoff high of 56 points together with 35 rebounds to lead his team to a victory and on to the Division Finals.

In the Division Finals, the Boston Celtics were again blocking Wilt Chamberlain's quest for basketball immortality. As good as Wilt was in the three years he had played in the NBA, he was yet to come close to winning a title since the Boston Celtics were a dynasty during the 1960's. Nobody could stop the Celtics. And while Chamberlain was an unstoppable force himself, Bill Russell was almost always there to be a thorn in his side. Russell was the only man that could contain and prevent Chamberlain from completely dominating the NBA during the 1960's. That 1962 series between the Warriors and Celtics was a renewal of a rivalry that started back in 1960. It was the second playoff meeting between the two best players of that era.

It was a hotly contested series throughout. No team gave an inch. Both the Warriors and the Celtics rode the high of their hometown crowds as they won each of their home games. It would take until Game 7 for a winner to finally be decided. Unfortunately for the Warriors, it had to be played on the home floor of the Celtics. Neither of the two teams had won a game against the opposing crowd all series long.

Game 7 was as close as any game could ever be played. The two teams traded jabs and defended each other well. Even Wilt Chamberlain struggled to score against the toughest defense that

Boston could put up. He only scored 22 that night. The final two points he scored was the basket he drained to tie the game up with only 16 seconds left in the match. However, he was helpless as the Celtics' Sam Jones made a basket that put the Celtics up by two with only two seconds left. That shot was enough to seal the Warriors' fate and send Chamberlain packing with no championship rings on any of his fingers.

Averaging 50 points an entire season but failing to win a title and to produce when it was most important made Wilt Chamberlain the subject of criticism after that loss to Boston. However, it could not be helped that he could win titles in the three years he spent in Philadelphia as a Warrior. The Warriors were only relying heavily on Chamberlain for the scoring and rebounding. While Paul Arizin was a capable player, he was getting old and was not as productive as he used to be. Chamberlain also lacked a quality big man along his side to help attract defenses away from him. That was the reason why the Warriors would often lose when the Big Dipper was struggling against opposing defenses. Chamberlain needed help and backup to the point that it did not matter anymore whether he would again average 50 points in an entire season.

The Move to San Francisco, Missing the Playoffs

During the offseason of 1962, Eddie Gottlieb sold the Warriors franchise to Marty Simmons, who was based in San Francisco.

Because of that, the team had to relocate all the way to the West Coast to become the San Francisco Warriors, which is now the Golden State Warriors. This meant that Wilt Chamberlain would have to play far away from his hometown for the first time in his NBA career.

What the move to San Francisco also meant that the Warriors had to break up the team that made the playoffs the last three seasons. Paul Arizin, the Warriors' secondary scorer, was not willing to move away from his family and day job. He chose to retire instead of leaving Philadelphia. On the other hand, Tom Gola would, later on, request a trade to New York after missing his home in Philadelphia in the middle of the season in San Francisco. All those factors led to what was then Wilt's worse season as a pro.

Without Paul Arizin, who himself is a Hall of Fame scorer, much of the offensive load was shouldered by Wilt Chamberlain. He would open the new season in San Francisco going for 56 points and 29 rebounds in a win over the Detroit Pistons on October 23, 1962. He followed that up three days later against the very same team by going for 50 points and 41 rebounds. Opening the season winning three straight for the Warriors, the Stilt went for 46 points and 23 rebounds against the Chicago Zephyrs on October 27.

On November 3, Wilt Chamberlain would go for his first 70-point game that season when he made 29 of his 48 field goals to score 72 markers in a loss to the Los Angeles Lakers. Two weeks later, he would top that performance by going for 73 points and 14 rebounds in a win against New York, where he made 29 of his 43 field goal attempts. However, that win against the Knicks turned out to be the last time in a long while that Wilt would taste what it was like to win games.

After that win against the New York Knicks on November 16, Wilt Chamberlain's San Francisco Warriors would lose 11 consecutive games. Not even a one-man wrecking crew like the Big Dipper could win games by himself. Basketball is a team sport, and not even the most dominant player could salvage an entire team from obscurity. Wilt Chamberlain averaged 48 points and 24.6 rebounds during that losing run. He scored at least 50 points six times during that run as opposing teams allowed him to score points while containing his teammates.

On December 11, Chamberlain would break that losing run by going for 61 points and 26 rebounds against the Syracuse Nationals. And though it came at a loss three days later, he scored 63 points against the Lakers. On December 18, he would score 61 points against the St. Louis Hawks to give another win for the San Francisco Warriors, who desperately needed to get back on the winning track.

The next time that Wilt Chamberlain would score at least 60 points was on January 11, 1963, against the Lakers. Dominating the paint, he would go for 67 points on a 60% shooting clip that night. But he could not do enough against a Laker team that had two all-time Hall of Fame greats in Jerry West and Elgin Baylor. The Warriors would end up losing that bout. At that time, wins became a rarity for Wilt's team. Never in his lifetime as a basketball player had Chamberlain tasted more losses than wins before that first season in San Francisco.

As a consolation of sorts for the Warriors, who were already out of contention for the playoffs, Wilt Chamberlain would go for another 70-point game on March 10. Making 71% of his 38 field goal attempts, Chamberlain scored 70 points, but his team still lost by 15 points to a Syracuse team he had faced in the playoffs the past three seasons.

However, there was not going to be a fourth-time straight season for Wilt's Warriors versus the Syracuse Nationals. San Francisco lost 49 games during the regular season and would miss the playoffs. With the team leaning heavily on his shoulders more than it ever did, Wilt the Stilt averaged 44.8 points and 24.3 rebounds that season. Though his efforts were for naught, his scoring average that season remains the second highest in NBA history after his 50.4 average the previous year. And while Wilt was still solidifying his name as the best individual player in the NBA and arguably league history, there was only so much he could do. He never won titles even with capable players back in Philadelphia. This time, without such players, he could not even make the playoffs all on his own.

Teaming With Nate Thurmond, First Finals Appearance

If there was a bright side to the San Francisco Warriors missing the playoffs the past season, it was that they got a high draft pick in the 1963 NBA Draft. With their third overall pick, they would decide to take the 6'11" center Nate Thurmond to pair him up with Wilt Chamberlain. Initially, Thurmond was Wilt's backup center. Eventually, he would develop into the Stilt's partner down in the paint as the pair formed one of the first of many dominant twin tower combinations in league history.

Aside from drafting Thurmond, one of the biggest additions that the Warriors had during the offseason was hiring a new head coach in the form of future Hall of Famer Alex Hannum. What made Hannum special was that he was not afraid of getting into Wilt's face because of his background as a military man. He also emphasized the importance of playing good defense rather than focusing on offense. He also made it a point to move the ball around instead of just freezing it in the hands of Wilt. Hannum would tell Chamberlain to pass the ball more often, especially when he was getting ganged up on. This led Wilt the Stilt to develop his ability as a passer.

With Wilt Chamberlain putting more effort on team basketball and defense, he was no longer putting up those enormous scoring numbers. The Warriors were playing at a slower pace than they did before because of their emphasis on defense. And while Chamberlain was still a dominant scorer, he would not have the eye-popping numbers he had the last two seasons.

Nevertheless, he still had great dominant performances. Early in the season, he went for 55 points, 29 rebounds, and six assists against the LA Lakers in a win on November 2, 1963. Then on November 13 against the Cincinnati Royals, he would go for 49 points and 22 rebounds in another win for the San Francisco Warriors. Six days later, he would display his newfound passing tendencies in an excellent all-around performance in a dominant win against the Hawks. He finished that night with 40 points, 20 rebounds, and nine assists.

On December 18, Wilt Chamberlain would have one of his many triple-doubles that season after going for 27 points, 27 rebounds, and 11 assists in a win over the St. Louis Hawks. And four days later against the newly relocated Philadelphia 76ers (formerly the Syracuse Nationals), the Big Dipper would dominate his old hometown team by going for another fantastic all-around performance. In another triple-double output, Wilt finished that win with 40 points, 23 rebounds, and 12 assists.

Several weeks later on January 28, 1964, Wilt Chamberlain would have another similar performance against the 76ers. This time it was in front of his hometown crowd. In that 22-point win against Philadelphia, the Stilt finished with a then season high of 59 points together with 13 rebounds and nine assists. Barely two weeks later, he would have 59 points again when he helped defeat the Detroit Pistons.

A week after scoring 59 against the Pistons, Chamberlain had another great night against Detroit. In what was his first 50-30 game that season, Wilt the Stilt finished a win with 52 points and 32 rebounds. That was just one night after he had 52 against the Cincinnati Royals in what was a disappointing loss for the San Francisco Warriors.

On March 7, Chamberlain would have another triple-double. In a win against the Lakers, he would go for 47 points, 13 rebounds, and ten assists. Just three days later, he would replicate that performance against another newly relocated team, the Baltimore Bullets (formerly the Chicago Zephyrs). Chamberlain finished that game with 32 points, 22 rebounds, and 13 dimes.

By the end of the season, Wilt Chamberlain averaged a league-leading 36.9 points, together with 22.3 rebounds, and a then-career high of 5 assists. The Stilt led the league in scoring for the fifth consecutive season, though he failed to lead the league in rebounds that year after four seasons of grabbing the most number of boards. Nevertheless, the new system and Chamberlain's new mentality made him a better passer.

The addition of Nate Thurmond also alleviated a lot of pressure off of Wilt Chamberlain. In his first four seasons, the Big Dipper was the only man worth defending near the basket. He never had a consistent big man tandem that could also attract defenders near the basket. It was always him getting ganged up on by multiple opponents when he was under the rim. However, with Thurmond around, Chamberlain had a near equally large teammate that could also score inside the paint and grab rebounds in bunches. Nate's defense also allowed the Warriors to own the middle of their side of the court as San Francisco became a fearsome defensive unit with two seven-footers patrolling near the bucket. Because of this, the Warriors improved their record to 48 wins.

With the Warriors leading the Western Division in wins that season, they had an automatic berth in the Division Finals where they would face off against the St. Louis Hawks for a chance to make it all the way to the NBA's championship series. This battle against the Hawks turned out to be a physical and intense matchup even for Chamberlain, who was used to the physicality of defenders during the playoffs.

In Game 1 of that Division Finals matchup, the Hawks managed to get the upper hand and were clicking on all cylinders. In contrast, Wilt Chamberlain was the only one on the Warriors' roster that could do any damage. He finished with 37 points and 22 rebounds, but his other teammates were nowhere to be found in that loss for San Francisco. But Game 2 was a different story when all the other supporting players were doing their job to help the dominant center. Chamberlain had 28 points, 27 rebounds, and five assists, but he was not alone in that blowout win for the Warriors.

In St. Louis for Game 3, the Hawks performed as well as they did in Game 1. Four players scored at least 20 points whereas the Big Dipper, who had 46 points and 23 rebounds, was a one-man show yet again for the San Francisco Warriors. Because of that, St. Louis got the upper hand and the series lead again. Fortunately, in Game 4, the Stilt had enough help and performed just as admirably himself to tie the series again. He finished that game with 36 points and 23 rebounds.

Wilt Chamberlain was at his best in Game 5 when he was virtually forcing his team to gain the series lead for the first time. Chamberlain was not only clicking from the field but was also helping his teammates in the process of what was eventually going to be a blowout win. Wilt finished that bout with 50 points, 15 rebounds, and six assists. Nevertheless, the Hawks would tie the series with a win in Game 6 and would force a deciding Game 7 to determine who was going to the NBA Finals.

Not willing to see his chance of making it all the way to the Finals for the very first time blow up like a bubble, Wilt Chamberlain put the team on his back on both ends of the floor. He was scoring, rebounding, and making plays at high rates, and nobody on the St. Louis Hawks' roster could neutralize him. In the end, Chamberlain led the way with 39 points, 30 rebounds, and six assists. Wilt brought the team to a win and his first ever appearance in the NBA Finals.

In the Finals, a familiar face donning the uniform of the most dominant team in league history was waiting for Chamberlain. At that time, Bill Russell was already a six-time NBA champion with the Boston Celtics. The Celtics had been the NBA's premier team and had been a dynasty for so long that no team had ever come close to toppling their dominant hold on the league. But Chamberlain was so used to breaking records. Was he the one to break the Celtics' record-setting championship streak? Only the Finals would tell that story as Wilt and Bill would once again renew the biggest rivalry among big men in league history.

Proving their dominance as the league's best team, the Boston Celtics thoroughly outplayed the San Francisco Warriors during the first two games of the series. Chamberlain himself struggled against Russell, who is regarded as arguably the greatest defender in league history. Russell held his own and denied the Stilt of the best position and the best look near the basket. Because of that, Wilt could not get up a shot he liked and struggled for only 22 points in Game 1 against the defensive specialist. In Game 2, he may have performed better, but his team was neutralized, and the Celtics took that one away by 23 points.

In Game 3 when the series moved over to San Francisco, it was the Warriors' turn to dominate the Celtics. Seemingly feeling the effects of the long travel, the Celtics could not get up a shot while everyone in a Warriors uniform was draining buckets. Of course, Chamberlain led the way with his 35 points, 25 rebounds, and five assists. It was all enough to give the team a 24-point win.

Games 4 and 5 were all hard fought compared to the first three games. None of the players relented an inch to their opposition. Russell was trying to hold his own against Chamberlain while all the other Celtics were doing their best to counter the offensive outburst that the Stilt was putting up. Despite scoring 27 points and grabbing 38 rebounds, Chamberlain could not lead his team to a win in Game 4. And in Game 5, the Celtics finally put them away to win their sixth consecutive NBA championship at the expense of the league's greatest individual player.

The narrative was the same for Wilt Chamberlain after that season. He was a monstrous player that broke record after record every season. He could win fans and awards over to his side, but the one thing he could never win at that point in his career was an NBA championship. Not even another capable big man in the form of Nate Thurmond could help him accomplish the only prize that had eluded him since his rookie season. At that point, only a change of scenery could help the Big Dipper win his very first NBA title.

Final Run With the Warriors, the Trade to Philadelphia

Right after that NBA Finals affair that Wilt Chamberlain had with Bill Russell, regarded one of the best big men in league history, he would find himself meeting another future all-time great center. During the offseason of 1964, Wilt would meet a young 17-year-old seven-footer named Lew Alcindor in the famed Rucker Park Tournament in New York. Impressed by the teenager, Chamberlain would even give Alcindor one of his best suits and would welcome the future Hall of Famer into his inner circle. Lew Alcindor would later become Kareem Abdul-Jabbar and the league's all-time leading scorer. Unfortunately, the relationship between the two all-time greats would diminish after they find themselves as rivals on the basketball court. But at that time, there was no arguing that the Stilt was the more accomplished player, especially with the way he was leading the Warriors.

While that Finals run that Wilt Chamberlain had with the San Francisco Warriors was anything but a miracle, it was only going to be a one-hit wonder as the following season would be a tumultuous one not only for the franchise, but also for the Big Dipper himself. The Warriors got off to a rough start to the 1964-65 season because of roster and financial problems.

Even with Wilt dominating early in the season, he could not do enough to lead his team out of obscurity. His early high-scoring game of 52 points against the Knicks on November 6, 1964, was sufficient for a win, but he would later find himself losing even after going for 53 points and 23 rebounds against the Detroit Pistons on November 12. Three days later, he would even go for 62 points and 22 rebounds against the Cincinnati Royals. However, the Warriors would go on to lose six straight games. That losing streak was capped off by his 63-

point and 32-rebound performance against the Philadelphia 76ers on November 26. Even with that performance, the Warriors lost.

Wilt Chamberlain continued such performances for the San Francisco Warriors even as the team continued to lose. He was carrying his team, though it was already becoming evident that he would not have the same run as he did the last season. Nevertheless, Wilt the Stilt was an All-Star for a sixth straight season. But that would be the final time he would do so as a Warrior.

On January 13, 1965, just after the All-Star Game, Wilt Chamberlain was announced to have been traded by the San Francisco Warriors to a familiar city and a familiar team. The Philadelphia 76ers took Wilt in by trading away Connie Dierking, Paul Newman, Lee Schaffer, and $150,000. While none of those players would carve out respectable NBA careers, the reason for the trade was the cash incentive that the Warriors would get considering the financial problems the franchise was facing. That was the primary factor for trading away the league's best individual player.

With the trade finalized, Wilt Chamberlain was finally going home to the city where he started basketball. It was also the city that first welcomed him as an NBA player back when the Warriors were still based in Philadelphia. This time, however, he was joining a team he has had clashes with in the past. The 76ers were used to be Syracuse Nationals, who Chamberlain's Warriors had met three straight seasons back when they were still in Philadelphia. The Big Dipper had memorable wars with Hal Greer, Larry Costello, and then-head coach Dolph Schayes. But with Chamberlain joining the 76ers, the former players he had been warring with back in the past were now his teammates.

After Chamberlain joined the 76ers, his new teammates began to realize that they had the best player in the world. Leaders such as Hal Greer and Larry Costello would make way for the big man as the new alpha of the team. Meanwhile, promising rookie All-Star center Luke Jackson moved to the power forward slot knowing that Chamberlain was going to be the main man in the middle. The only person in the franchise that Wilt the Stilt had problems with was head coach Dolph Schayes because of the many derogatory remarks the latter had made towards the Big Dipper when they were still bitter rivals a few seasons before.

On January 21, 1965, Wilt Chamberlain made his 76ers debut against no less than his former team, the San Francisco Warriors. Playing for a familiar crowd against an equally familiar team, Chamberlain dominated the defensive end of the floor. He collected 29 rebounds and had 22 points in his 76ers debut. The Sixers finished that game with a win.

With talented scorers and teammates flanking and backing him up, Wilt Chamberlain never had to dominate the possessions and scoring opportunities. He would even fail to score over 40 points in his first 16 games with the 76ers. But on February 18 in a loss to the Lakers,

Wilt the Stilt would finally score 40 after hitting 17 of his 29 field goals. Three days later, he replicated the performance in a win over the Baltimore Bullets.

On March 5 in a win against the Cincinnati Royals, Wilt Chamberlain would go for a new high as a Sixer by going for 48 points together with 22 rebounds. A night later, he would even go for 43 rebounds against the Celtics and Bill Russell. The Stilt would top his Sixer high that season by going for 51 points in a loss to the Bullets on March 14.

Wilt Chamberlain would end the regular season leading the NBA in scoring for the sixth straight season. He averaged 34.7 points together with 22.9 rebounds. His scoring numbers took a dip after he moved to Philadelphia. He was averaging 39 points in San Francisco but went on to score 30 points a night with the 76ers. Nevertheless, he was the reason the Philadelphia 76ers made the playoffs with a 40-40 record.

In the Division Semi-Finals, the Philadelphia 76ers quickly dispatched the Cincinnati Royals in four games even though Wilt Chamberlain was not putting up great numbers. Against the Royals, the Stilt averaged 27.8 points, 20 rebounds, and 6.3 assists. It was mainly because of how well his teammates were picking up the slack that led to the 76ers easily defeating the Royals.

In the Division Finals, it was once again a renewal of the rivalry between Chamberlain and Russell when the Sixers met the Celtics for a second straight season in the playoffs. This time, however, Wilt was coming into their bout with better teammates and more experience as a leader. This series also showed how Chamberlain emphasized more on defense and rebounding rather than scoring.

Once again, it was a physical paint battle between Chamberlain and Russell. Wilt and Bill battled on the boards, and both players were eating up rebounds in a defensive battle. Chamberlain finished that game with 33 points and 31 rebounds. Meanwhile, Russell had 32 rebounds. However, the Celtics finished that bout with a win. Game 2 was a little different. Chamberlain was dominant in all facets of the matchup. He had 30 points, 39 big rebounds, and even finished with eight assists in a game where all of the other Sixers players were clicking. Philadelphia ended that night with a win to tie the series.

The Sixers and the Celtics would also split the next four games to force a seventh and deciding game after the series was tied at 3-3. Coming into Game 7, the mammoth of a man named Wilt Chamberlain was averaging 30.2 points and 31 rebounds. And from Games 1 to 4, he was even norming 30 points and 35 boards. But none of that would matter unless Wilt finished the series with a win against Bill and his Celtics.

In Game 7, none team gave an inch. It would take until the final play of the game to decide a winner and finalist. With five seconds left in the game, Chamberlain was clutch and scored four straight points on free throws and a dunk to cut the Celtics' lead to a solitary point. The 76ers then had another chance to win the game when Bill Russell botched an inbound pass.

Down merely a point, head coach Dolph Schayes drew a play for Hal Greer because he believed that Wilt Chamberlain would be fouled. He was not willing to take the chance of the Big Dipper missing his free throws. However, it turned out to be a bad call on Schayes' part. Greer made a bad inbound pass that led to one of history's greatest moments. The Celtics' John Havlicek stole the ball and held on to the possession to give Boston another win. Once again, Russell was a title holder for the eighth time in his career while Chamberlain was still without a ring. This was the first time Wilt heard criticisms about his ability to win titles and his capacity as a leader. Was Wilt Chamberlain just a dominant star that could not perform and win when it mattered most?

At that time, Chamberlain was not to blame for his losses. Though he was the single best star in the league at that point and was already arguably the best player in the NBA's history, there were also star players that could win titles, not because they were losers, but because the Celtics were just unbeatable. Players such as Oscar Robertson, Elgin Baylor, and Jerry West were considered amongst the best players in the league but were also ringless because of the Boston Celtics, who have won eight of the nine last championships. In essence, Wilt was not alone as a player that could not win titles.

Second MVP, Another Celtics Loss

If there was anything Wilt Chamberlain could be happy about the trade to the Philadelphia 76ers, it was that he had better teammates in a better franchise compared to when he was still with the Warriors. It was during this season that he began to see more team success in his career while also putting up huge numbers for himself. Joined by teammates Hal Greer, Chet Walker, Luke Jackson, and promising rookie Billy Cunningham, the Big Dipper would find it easier to focus on defense, playmaking, and defense rather than putting all of his eggs on the scoring end.

Wilt Chamberlain started the 1965-66 season with a 32-point win against the Baltimore Bullets on October 16, 1965. He had 33 points and 25 rebounds that night. A week later in his second game, the Big Dipper had a then-season high of 53 points in a win over the Detroit Pistons. Another week later, he led the Sixers to a 3-0 season start by going for a triple-double game of 39 points, 28 rebounds, and ten assists. As evidenced by his great early start, Wilt Chamberlain was more focused on rebounding and making plays for his teammates more than he ever did.

The next time Wilt the Stilt had a triple-double was on December 15 against the Los Angeles Lakers. He had 31 points, 23 rebounds, and 13 assists that night. Two days later, he nearly had another one after going for 38 points, 24 rebounds, and nine assists against the very same Laker team. Several days later on December 28, he finished with 31 points, six assists, and a then-season high of 40 rebounds against the Boston Celtics.

On January 14, 1966, Wilt Chamberlain would exceed his season high in rebounds. In a win against the Boston Celtics, he was once again a monster on the boards. The Big Dipper went for 42 rebounds on top of the 37 points and six assists that he had in that dominant effort. And in his very next game, he had an equally monstrous performance by going for 44 points, 23 rebounds, and eight assists.

Wilt would then tie his season high in points later on January 25 against the Los Angeles Lakers. He had 53 points and 31 rebounds in that win. But Wilt was not done, because a few weeks later on February 7, Chamberlain would go for a new season high. The Big Dipper made 28 of his 43 field goals that night against the Lakers. He finished with 65 points and 29 rebounds.

When the season was nearing its end, Wilt began passing more and collecting more triple-doubles. He had six more triple-doubles to end the regular season. The best of which was when he had 41 points, 23 rebounds, and 13 assists in a win over the Pistons on February 14. But Chamberlain would later show that he was at his best when he was shooting the ball.

On March 3 against his old team the San Francisco Warriors, Wilt Chamberlain was out of his mind. Showing the Warriors that it was a bad decision to trade him away for money, Wilt finished with a 26 out of 39 shooting clip from the field and finished with 62 points and 37 big rebounds. The Sixers won that game with Chamberlain dominating his old team.

By the end of the season, Wilt Chamberlain finished the regular season leading the league in both points and rebounds. He averaged

33.5 points, 24.6 rebounds, and 5.2 assists. He also led the league in field goal shooting after making 54% of his shots. And because of how he led the Sixers to a 55-25 season to finish with the top seed in the East, Chamberlain was awarded his second MVP award six seasons after winning his first one.

Coming into the Division Finals against the Celtics once again, Chamberlain had home court advantage for the first time in his career against Boston. However, the advantage did not matter. The league MVP leading the best team in the league during the regular season would fall to the perennial champions in only five games. This once again led people to criticize Chamberlain, not because he could not win, but because it was his selfish desires that prevented his team from winning.

One of the biggest selfish act that Wilt was often criticized for was the fact that he decided to live in New York rather than Philadelphia. Chamberlain was always a late sleeper because of how much he enjoyed the New York nightlife. And being from New York, he would have to travel to Philadelphia for practices. This led Dolph Schayes to move practices to the afternoon to the dismay of other players who wanted the time off late in the day. But Wilt, despite pleas from teammates and coaches, did not want to move to Philadelphia.[viii]

During the 1966 Division Finals against the Celtics, Chamberlain showed his selfish side once again when he decided to skip practice because he was too tired after winning Game 3 of that series. The Sixers would lose Game 4. And before Game 5, again, he would skip practice.[viii] Despite performing well in Game 5, his teammates could not sway their focus away from Wilt's selfish acts. This led to the loss of the Sixers at the hands of the Celtics in only five games.

Third MVP, First NBA Championship

In response to Dolph Schayes, who was forgiving and less confrontational with Wilt Chamberlain, the Philadelphia 76ers decided to fire the head coach to install a familiar face named Alex Hannum. Hannum was responsible for coaching Wilt Chamberlain to his only playoff season back in San Francisco during the 1963-64 season. What he emphasized back then was making his star center a better passer. The same philosophy was not lost when he moved to Philadelphia.

Hannum was never afraid of getting into Wilt's face. There were even moments when teammates had to break the two apart when they would nearly trade fists with one another. However, this only led to Chamberlain respecting his head coach more than he ever had in his entire life. And when the two men realized they were on the same page, the Big Dipper bought into Hannum's philosophy of making him a dominant all-around player that focused on ball movement and efficient shots rather than giving him every possible possession and scoring opportunity.

Perfectly buying into his coach's belief, Wilt came into the season focusing on defense and distributing possessions amongst equally talented players such as Greer, Walker, Jackson, and Cunningham. Six Sixers players were averaging double figures in scoring that season because of how well they distributed the ball. Chamberlain even focused all of his scoring prowess into making sure he had the best shot opportunities.

The 76ers started the season winning seven straight games without a loss. In those seven games, Wilt the Stilt only scored at least 30 points once. That was when he had 30 points, 26 rebounds, and 13 assists in their seventh straight win, which was against the San Francisco Warriors. He even shot 72% from the floor in that game.

On November 11, 1966, Wilt had his new season high in points against the newly formed Chicago Bulls. He finished that night with 37 points, 33 rebounds, and seven assists while shooting well over 78% from the field. He would then lead his team to six more wins to finish an eight-game winning streak. He would flirt with triple-doubles during that run, but would finally win against the Royals on November 19. He had 20 points, 17 rebounds, and 11 assists in that win.

Wilt Chamberlain showed that he was still a dominant scorer if he wanted to be. On November 25, Wilt the Stilt had 41 points while missing only one of his 17 shots. He finished that night with 19 rebounds when he led the Sixers to a win against the Baltimore

Bullets. A night later against the Detroit Pistons, he would have 26 points, 24 rebounds, and 15 assists for another triple-double.

During a six-game run from December 16 to 26, Wilt Chamberlain would even average a triple-double in leading his team to what would eventually become ten straight wins. During that run, he averaged 24.2 points, 25.7 rebounds, and 10.8 assists. Wilt had five triple-doubles during that stretch.

Much later during February and March of 1967, Wilt Chamberlain had another similar run. In a span of 10 games, he averaged 22 points, 26 rebounds, and 10.6 assists. The Sixers would lose only one of those 10 games. In two of those games, he hardly attempted to score. He had 15 points, 22 rebounds, and 17 assists against Cincinnati on February 17. Then, on March 5, he had 10 points, 25 rebounds, and 16 assists. With performances like those, it had become apparent that the Sixers were a lot better when Chamberlain was moving the ball around.

During that 1966-67 season, Wilt Chamberlain averaged 24.1 points, 24.2 rebounds, and 7.8 assists. He led the league in rebounding, and for the first time since his rookie season, he would not finish the season as the top scorer. But because Wilt focused on scoring efficient buckets, he had a then-NBA record of 68% shooting from the field. While his scoring averages were a far cry from his best scoring seasons, Wilt Chamberlain was still named the league MVP after leading his team to a then NBA all-time best 68-13 record.

The NBA implemented a new playoff system during that season. All eight playoff teams would have to play all three series instead of giving a bye to the top-seeded squad. Because of this, the 76ers would square off in the Division Semis despite securing the league's then all-time best record. But it did not matter much considering that Philadelphia finished off Cincinnati in four games. In those four games, Wilt averaged 28 points, 26.5 rebounds, and 11 assists. His best performance was in Game 3 when he had 16 points, 30 rebounds, and 19 assists.

In the Division Finals, the Philadelphia 76ers would face the Boston Celtics for the third straight season. And for the second year in a row, the Sixers had home court advantage. Despite losing last season, Wilt now had a much better grip on his abilities and role with the team. This was no longer the Stilt that tried to win games on his own. This time, Chamberlain had become a much better leader and player as far as the team aspect of the game was concerned.

Wilt Chamberlain immediately made it known that he was tired of losing to the Boston Celtics. In Game 1, Wilt focused more on defense and passing the ball. He finished the game with 24 points while shooting only 13 attempts. He then had a tripled-double by going for 32 rebounds and 13 assists. And if history is correct, he even had a quadruple-double after tallying 12 unofficial blocks. Back then, blocks were not counted officially by the NBA, so officially, he only had a triple-double in that win.

Chamberlain would have similar performances in Games 2 and 3. No longer did Bill Russell have to defend Wilt's ability to score. This time, the entire team forced themselves to become wary of the Big Dipper's ability to make plays for his teammates. While Chamberlain only had 15 points and 29 rebounds, he still came out with a win in Game 2. Then in Game 3, he had 20 points, 41 rebounds, and nine assists.

After losing Game 4 despite his second triple-double that series, Wilt Chamberlain went into Game 5 focused on exorcising his Celtics demons. Playing all facets of the game at an elite level, Wilt the Stilt finished the game with 29 points, 36 rebounds, and 13 assists. That performance was the biggest reason for that blowout win in favor of the Sixers. Because of that, Chamberlain ended the eight-year run of the Boston Celtics as champions. In effect, he finally defeated Bill Russell in the playoffs. He would also earn his eternal rival's praise because of his performance during the series.

Beating Russell and the Celtics was not the high point of Chamberlain's season. He still had to go to the NBA Finals for the second time in his career to have another chance at his first championship. This time, it was against a familiar franchise. The San Francisco Warriors had found success by building around Nate Thurmond and talented all-time great scorer Rick Barry. If Wilt wanted to win a title that season, he would have to beat his old team to do so.

In Game 1, Chamberlain was intent on putting everything on the line for that elusive NBA championship. He would lead the Sixers to an overtime win by going for 16 points, 33 rebounds, and ten assists. Interestingly, the once 50-point scorer only took eight shots that night. In Game 2 when the Sixers won dominantly, Wilt took over on the all-around aspects of the game once again. Going for ten points, 38 rebounds, and 10 assists, the Sixers went on to a 2-0 lead to open the series.

Game 3 showed that it was a bad idea for Wilt Chamberlain to try to focus on scoring. He took 26 shots and made more than half of them to score 26 points. He also had 26 rebounds. However, the Warriors rallied to win that game in San Francisco. Then in Game 4, the Big Dipper would take only six shots to finish with 10 points on top of 27 rebounds and eight assists in what was a win for the Sixers. Up 3-1, it did not matter that the Warriors won Game 5.

In a tightly contested Game 6, Wilt Chamberlain and the Sixers would win the game on the strength of a final defensive play. Using the pick-and-roll to try to score a basket that would have put them up, the Warriors relied on Barry and Thurmond. However, the Sixers foiled the play by making sure they had a man on Barry after he freed himself up through Thurmond's pick.[viii] Chet Walker never gave the scorer an inch as the Philadelphia held on to their lead to win the NBA title for the second time in franchise history and for the first time since relocating from Syracuse.

By winning a title that season, Wilt Chamberlain could finally claim that he was a champion and a certified winner. The Big Dipper would argue that he had just become a part of history by leading the best team in NBA history all the way to the title. At that time, he was right in claiming that the 1966-67 Philadelphia 76ers were the best team in league history. Not only did they secure the all-time best record in the NBA at that time, but they also finished the season off with a championship. At the helm of it all was Wilt Chamberlain, who changed the way he played so that he could lead his team to a win.

Final Season in Philadelphia, Leading the League in Assists

Chamberlain's offseason could not have gotten off to a worse start, especially after he had just won an NBA title. The Big Dipper would find himself in a misunderstood situation with the only surviving owner of the Philadelphia 76ers, Irv Kosloff. For Wilt's case, he claimed to have a previous understanding with one of the late co-owners of the franchise saying that he would own a fourth of the team's shares after his career was over. Several reputable sources would even say that Wilt was right. However, Kosloff decided not to respect the agreement. This led Chamberlain to threaten ownership that he would switch to the ABA, the NBA's rival team. But the two would eventually settle a truce, at least for one season.[viii]

Wanting to win one more NBA title especially after he had already tasted what it was like to be a champion, Wilt Chamberlain would come into the 1967-68 season with the same kind of mindset he had the last season. This time, he came in wanting to pass the ball more than he ever did. No other center in league history was moving the ball like Wilt was that season.

Early on, Wilt the Stilt was already putting up triple-doubles. The first one he had was when he helped beat the Lakers on October 21, 1967, by putting up 17 points, 22 rebounds, and ten assists. Eleven days later, he would go for 19 points, 22 rebounds, and 13 assists. On November 4, Wilt did not even attempt a single shot from the floor when he went for 18 rebounds and 13 assists. The solitary point he had in that game came from a foul shot. It would even take ten games for the Big Dipper to score at least 20 points because of how he was passing the ball more than he shot it. This was a far cry from the Wilt Chamberlain that used to shoot 30% of his team's shots to score 50 points a game.

On November 24, Wilt Chamberlain would score at least 30 points for the first time. In that win against the Chicago Bulls, he had 34 points and 29 rebounds. Then, on December 1, he would explode for what was then a rare high-scoring game for him. The 31-year-old Chamberlain would go for 22 out of 29 from the floor to score 52 points in addition to the 37 rebounds he had in that win against a newly-formed Seattle SuperSonics team.

Wilt Chamberlain would suddenly top that performance. On December 16 against the Chicago Bulls, Wilt Chamberlain would make 30 of his 40 shots to score 68 points. He also had 34 rebounds in that win. Just a night later, he would go for 47 points and 26 rebounds against the Sonics. Against the very same team three days later, he had 53 points and 38 rebounds to finish off a three-game stretch where he averaged 56 points and 32.7 rebounds. Those three games proved that Wilt could still go for huge scoring games whenever he wanted to and whenever there was a need for him to do so.

Wilt the Stilt would even go on stretches where he would seemingly do everything on the floor at elite levels. Late in January until early February of 1968, he went for five straight triple-double performances. The best game he had in that stretch was when he had 22 points, 25 rebounds, and 21 assists for the NBA's first and only 20-20-20 triple-double game. That happened on February 2 in a win against the Detroit Pistons. No other player in league history has gotten close to putting up a similar output.

As the season was winding down, Wilt Chamberlain would top his five-game triple-double streak. In that stretch, Chamberlain would go for nine straight triple-doubles where he averaged 26.7 points, 23.7 rebounds, and 12.2 assists. The best he had during that streak was on March 18 against the Los Angeles Lakers. In that game, the Big Dipper had what was then the highest scoring triple-double game in league history. He had 53 points, 32 rebounds, and 14 assists in that match. It would take until 2017 for a player to break that record when Russell Westbrook had 57 points in a triple-double effort.

Rumors would even say that on that night of March 18, 1968, Wilt Chamberlain had a quintuple-double of 53 points, 32 rebounds, 14 assists, 24 blocks, and 11 steals. However, there was no way of telling whether he had 24 blocks and 11 steals that night considering that the NBA was not even tallying blocks and steals during those years. But considering how monstrous Wilt was on the defensive end of the court, he could very well have also compiled such numbers.

When the regular season was done, Wilt Chamberlain was once again the MVP for a third consecutive season after leading the 76ers to 62 wins. He was averaging 24.3 points, 23.8 rebounds, and 8.6 assists. For the first and only time in league history, a center led the entire NBA in assists. Only Wilt Chamberlain has ever been able to do that. No other big men in the league would even lead the league in assists. The Big Dipper is also the only player to have ever become a leader in points, rebounds, and assists in different seasons. If he wanted to score, he would score big. If he wanted to lead the league in rebounds, he would do so. And if he wanted to be the greatest point guard in the league, Chamberlain could easily become one. Wilt the Stilt did anything he wanted to do when he was on the court.

Wilt Chamberlain's quest for his second title started against the New York Knicks. He opened up the Philadelphia 76ers' championship defense by going for 37 points, 29 rebounds, and seven assists in a win. However, the Sixers would go on to lose Game 2 as the Knicks tied the series. The two teams would then split the next two games as the series was 2-2 heading into Game 5.

In Games 5 and 6, however, Wilt Chamberlain and his Sixers would not allow the Knicks one more game. Philadelphia would blow New York out in both those games to give Wilt the Stilt another Eastern Division Finals appearance against the Boston Celtics. In the Division Semis, Chamberlain averaged 25.5 points, 24.2 rebounds, and 6.3 assists.

Against the Celtics in that series, the Sixers would lose Game 1, but would go on to win three straight games to go up 3-1. Before that series, no NBA game has ever come back from a 1-3 deficit to win it all. It already seemed as if Wilt was heading to his second straight NBA Finals appearance. He would have even won another title.

However, the Celtics rallied to their defense to force all of the 76ers' players to shoot poorly from the field. Wilt Chamberlain also struggled to get his touches from the post in the final three games of the series as Alex Hannum himself admitted he should have given the ball to his star player more often. This ultimately led to the Boston Celtics winning three straight games to win the series. They would eventually win another NBA title that year.

With that loss to the Celtics during the 1968 playoffs, Wilt Chamberlain fell to 1-6 against Bill Russell in postseason series. It was that lone victory in 1967 that delivered him his first and only NBA title that time. And although Wilt had been successful with the Sixers the last two seasons thanks in large part to his change of mentality and to his head coach, the Big Dipper had played his final game for Philadelphia in that Game 7 loss to the Celtics.

The Move to LA

After the 1968 season, Alex Hannum would move to the ABA because he wanted to coach somewhere close to his home. This was led to what would eventually become a trade that Wilt Chamberlain himself requested. On July 9, 1968, Wilt the Stilt was moved over to Los Angeles to play for the Lakers in exchange for Darrall Imhoff, Jerry Chambers, and Archie Clark.

There are several rumored reasons as to why Wilt Chamberlain requested the trade to LA. He felt offended after the Sixers ownership refused to grant him that 25% share he was previously promised. Another probable reason was that Chamberlain was threatening to go over to the ABA to follow Hannum, the only coach he has had success with in the NBA. Finally, some would say that the Big Dipper felt that he had outgrown Philadelphia and that he wanted to go over to Los Angeles where all the celebrities were and where the culture was much more liberated.[viii] But whatever the reason was, Wilt Chamberlain was finally a Laker.

Wilt Chamberlain was slated to join a Los Angeles Lakers team that had two all-time greats and two of the top five players of that era. Elgin Baylor was the established alpha of that team after spending more than a decade in LA putting up ridiculous stats, much like how Wilt did back when he was a Warrior. Meanwhile, Jerry West was the

Lakers' top scorer, perimeter hotshot, and floor leader. It was a team built around three of the best players of that era despite the fact that they were already aging stars.

Despite the fact that Wilt Chamberlain was the league's best superstar and the NBA's all-time best player at that time, not everything went smoothly. Reports were saying that the Big Dipper was not a natural leader in LA and that he was often seen arguing with Baylor. The worst part of everything was that he had a poor relationship with then-Lakers head coach Butch van Breda Kolff, who would often bench him and criticize him for being too selfish, especially when it came to his statistics. The Laker head coach also cared more for Baylor and West rather than Wilt, who was just as big of a star as those two were.

Despite that, Wilt Chamberlain still had great performances in what was a tumultuous first year in Los Angeles. On January 26, 1969, he had a then-season high of 60 points in addition to 21 rebounds in a win against the Cincinnati Royals. Several weeks later on February 9, he topped that off by going for 66 points and 27 rebounds against the Phoenix Suns, the NBA's newest team that season.

Wilt Chamberlain would end the regular season with 20.5 points, 21.5 rebounds, and 4.5 assists. For the first time in his career, he did not lead his team in points. Nevertheless, the Los Angeles Lakers won 55 games as opposed to the 27 losses they had that season. The Lakers would finish the season as the top seed in the Western Division.

Against Wilt Chamberlain's old team the San Francisco Warriors, the LA Lakers would lose the first two games of the Division Semi-Finals. However, they would proceed to win the next four games to advance to the Division Finals. During that series, it was clear that Wilt did not have his coach's favor. His touches were limited, and he would only average 12 points in that series. The same was true when the Lakers defeated the Atlanta Hawks in five games in the Division Finals. Despite not playing like he was the best player in the world, Chamberlain was more than happy enough that he was heading to his third NBA Finals.

For the second time in his career, Wilt Chamberlain would face Bill Russell in the NBA Finals. This time, however, he had home court advantage compared to when he was still a Warrior in 1964. He also had better star teammates in 1969 as opposed to 1964, though he was already a different player with different tendencies in his second Finals meeting with Russell.

The series started out well for the Lakers. Chamberlain had 15 points and 23 rebounds to win Game 1 at home in Los Angeles. Then, in Game 2, he focused more on defense and rebounding to finish the game with 19 rebounds and only 4 points. Nevertheless, the Los Angeles Lakers won that game to start the series out 2-0. But in Boston, the Lakers would lose two straight as the Celtics tied the series 2-2.

In Game 5, Wilt Chamberlain had 13 points and 31 rebounds in a game where Baylor and West had to carry the heavy load. The Lakers would win that game to go up 3-2. But that would be their final win during the Finals. After losing Game 6, the Lakers came back strong in the last quarter of Game 7 despite trailing for much of the match. Then the unfortunate happened.

Trailing by a single point with three minutes left in the game, Wilt Chamberlain twisted his knee and had to be taken out of the match. Without the Big Dipper, the Lakers struggled to get the all-around production that Wilt had at the center position. This ultimately led to the Lakers' demise in seven games at the hand of the Boston Celtics. For the sixth time since 1962, the Los Angeles Lakers would lose at the hands of the Boston Celtics in the NBA Finals. But as a consolation of sorts, Jerry West was named the inaugural Finals MVP that year.

Wilt Chamberlain became the target of criticisms once again. Bill Russell himself thought that the Big Dipper's injury was not even grave enough to keep him out in the most crucial stretch of that Finals game. This led to Chamberlain earning the reputation as a player that refused to take over when he was needed and as a selfish and lazy star that would not want to fight with his team during the most important stretches.[viii]

The Injury Season, More Finals Woes

In his second season with the Lakers during the 1969-70 campaign, Wilt Chamberlain saw more touches on the offensive end because of the new head coach that LA had hired. Early in the season, he had scored 30 or more points six times and had two games of scoring at least 40 points. Unfortunately, he would suffer a severe knee injury that kept him out for almost the entire season. He only played nine games at that juncture, averaging 32.2 points. He would return four months later on March 18 to play the Lakers' final three games. He averaged 27.3 points, 18.4 rebounds, and 4.1 assists during that season.

The highlight of what was a short regular season for Wilt Chamberlain happened on October 24, 1969. It was a game between the LA Lakers and the Milwaukee Bucks. The then 33-year-old Big Dipper would meet 22-year-old 7'2" rookie center Lew Alcindor, who was slated to become the next big thing and the heir apparent for the position of the league's best center. Despite facing a younger player, Wilt owned the future Abdul-Jabbar by going for 25 points as opposed to 23 markers from Alcindor in that Laker win.

Despite missing Chamberlain for the majority of the regular season, the LA Lakers won 46 games to make the playoffs. They would start their journey to the NBA Finals against the Phoenix Suns, who made their playoff debut that season. After winning Game 1, the Lakers would lose the next three games in the Division Semis to go down 1-3 in just four matches.

After failing to defend a 3-1 lead a few seasons back, Wilt was now in the position to make his comeback. With 36 points and 14 rebounds in Game 5, Chamberlain helped the Lakers to come within one game close to tying the Suns' series lead. While he would not score big in Game 6, Chamberlain finished with a triple-double of 12 points, 26 rebounds, and 11 assists to tie the series up and force Game 7. In the series clincher, he had 30 points and 27 rebounds in what was a dominant win for the Los Angeles Lakers. The Lakers would then secure an NBA Finals berth by sweeping the Hawks in the Division Finals.

The NBA Finals was a battle between the two biggest markets in the NBA. It was the Lakers of Los Angeles against the Knicks of New York City. While the Lakers had three future Hall of Famers of their own, New York had four of their own in the likes of Willis Reed, Dave DeBusschere, Bill Bradley, and Walt Frazier. The most prominent of the Knicks' players that time, Willis Reed, was predicted to be a tough mismatch for Wilt Chamberlain. While Wilt was a lot bigger and stronger, Reed was an excellent perimeter shooter.[viii] This meant that Chamberlain would be forced outside of his comfort zone near the basket. And at that time, the Big Dipper had just recovered from a knee injury that robbed him of much of the lateral quickness and speed that he used to dominate the game back in his younger years. The prediction was that he would struggle to defend against Reed's jumpers.

Game 1 was proof that Wilt was going to struggle against Reed. Willis Reed would go for 37 points as Chamberlain could not defend against his high post shots. New York would take that game by 12 points. In Game 2 however, Chamberlain had 19 points and 24 rebounds to tie the series and to take home court advantage away from the Knicks.

In Game 3, both teams played to a stalemate. It would take a miraculous shot from Jerry West, who hit a 60-foot heave, to tie the game up and to force overtime. Unfortunately, the Knicks took that bout in the extra period. But the Lakers would tie the series again in Game 4 on the strength of Wilt Chamberlain's 18 points, 25 rebounds, and seven assists.

Willis Reed would pull a thigh muscle in Game 5 and would miss the remainder of the match. While Wilt Chamberlain should have taken over at that point especially because he was much larger than the Knicks' backup centers, New York played aggressive team defense to frustrate the Big Dipper and to take the game away from the Lakers. But with Reed nowhere to be found in Game 6, Wilt Chamberlain dominated under the basket in a blowout win in favor of the Lakers. Wilt the Stilt finished that game with 45 points and 27 rebounds.

With Reed seemingly out of the all-important Game 7, it was almost an assurance that the Lakers would win their first title since relocating to Los Angeles. Wilt was also seemingly on his way to securing his second NBA title ring. However, Willis Reed inspired the New York crowd and the Knicks' roster by returning in Game 7 hobbling down the court and scoring the first four baskets of the match. The Knicks had built a lead too big for the Lakers to threaten them. This led to New York beating Los Angeles by 14 points in Game 7. Once again, Chamberlain lost another Game 7.

And once again, Wilt Chamberlain came under strict scrutiny because he was unable to take advantage of Reed's injury and because he failed to once again show up in Game 7. However, in his defense, Wilt himself had just made a comeback from a devastating knee injury that robbed him of his athleticism and his mobility.[viii] He had all the reasons to miss the entire season or even retire, but he did not do so because he still wanted to win a title for LA.

Losing to Kareem

Wilt came back healthy for the 1970-71 season, though he was already past his prime and was not as quick and or athletic as he used to be because of the injuries and wear and tear of his age and the many physical plays he had to endure since 1959. The Big Dipper came into the season with the same kind of role he played the last season. He focused mainly on defense and rebounding while making sure he was attempting only the most efficient shots.

Despite not being as offensively dominant as he used to be, Wilt Chamberlain would still put up high scoring numbers from time to time. In a loss to the Royals on January 1, 1971, he had 41 points for his first and only game of scoring at least 40 markers that season. And throughout the season, he had at least 30 points 14 different times while the offense was mostly revolving around Jerry West and LA returnee Gail Goodrich.

Chamberlain would average impressive numbers of 20.7 points, 18.2 rebounds, and 4.3 assists. And for the ninth time in his career, the 35-year-old Big Dipper led the league in rebounding. The Los Angeles Lakers would make the playoffs with 48 wins as opposed to 34 losses. What ruined their chances at a higher winning mark was Elgin Baylor's career-ending injury early in the season. He was forced to retire abruptly. Nevertheless, the Los Angeles Lakers were still one of the top contenders in the Western Division.

In the Western Conference Semi-finals, Wilt Chamberlain and the Lakers went up against the Chicago Bulls, who gave them a tough fight though LA won the first two games. The Bulls would go on to win both of their games in Chicago as home court advantage proved crucial for the Lakers and the Bulls. During Game 7 in LA, Wilt Chamberlain nearly had a triple-double effort to lead the Lakers past the Bulls. He finished with 25 points, 19 rebounds, and nine assists in that 11-point win.

In the West Finals, however, Wilt Chamberlain would have to deal with the biggest threat to his legacy as a center. Just two seasons after Bill Russell retired from the game of basketball, a young center was trying to make his name as the next big skyscraper in the NBA. The 24-year-old Lew Alcindor, now known as Kareem Abdul-Jabbar, was just awarded the MVP award after leading the NBA in scoring that season. At that point, there was almost no arguing that he had grown into the best center and best player in the game while Chamberlain's age was getting to him.

While both Wilt and Kareem were nearly as tall as each other, their styles could not have been more different. Chamberlain was a power player that relied on his strength and 300-pound frame. He used his athletic prowess and his superior size inside under the basket to bully defenders for easy baskets and power dunks.

On the other hand, Abdul-Jabbar was taller and longer but lankier. What he lacked in strength he more than made up for with his finesse as a scorer. Kareem Abdul-Jabbar used a variety of post moves that ranged from turnaround jumpers to spin moves near the basket. But the shot that made him an invincible scorer was the skyhook. He mastered that shot so well that it served him for two decades in the NBA and would make him the league's all-time leading scorer when it was all said and done. But at that point, he was still making a name for himself. One of the best ways to do so was to go through Wilt Chamberlain, who was then regarded as the greatest player the league had ever seen.

The series started in Milwaukee, and Abdul-Jabbar immediately made the older but more experienced Chamberlain work hard on both ends of the floor. Wilt struggled to defend the younger center, who would finish with 32 points as opposed to his 22. In effect, the Bucks easily won that game. But Chamberlain would answer the challenge of the future Laker center. He would score 26 points to outscore the 22 that Abdul-Jabbar had in that match. Nevertheless, the Bucks still came out with the win.

In Game 3, things turned for the worse when backup guard Keith Erickson went down with an injury. Despite that, Wilt Chamberlain still managed to hold his own against the younger center. He would lead the Lakers to victory by going for 24 points and 24 rebounds. But the Bucks would later win the next two games in blowout fashion to end the Lakers' playoff run. Despite the loss, Wilt was able to show that he could hold his own against the man considered the best player at that time. He was old and ailing with injuries and yet was able to make Kareem work.[viii] Abdul-Jabbar would eventually win his first NBA title season.

Second NBA Title

In the offseason of 1971, the Lakers hired Bill Sharman to be their new head coach. Sharman used to be a Celtics that played alongside Bill Russell. Impressively, he was able to transform Wilt into an entirely different player. Sharman would ask Chamberlain to be the Lakers' "Bill Russell." Throughout Russell's career, he was never the primary scoring option. He was the leader that focused on the defensive end of the floor while also making sure he was moving the ball around more. Russell was always a low-scoring pivot player that relied more on his leadership and defensive skills. Sharman embarked on turning Chamberlain into the same player.[viii]

Chamberlain would buy into the idea of becoming Bill Russell. He relished playing the defensive end of the floor to perfection while distributing the ball to the Lakers' hotshot backcourt duo of Jerry West and Gail Goodrich. Rarely did Wilt even try to take games over with his offense. He relied more on the defensive skills that made him one of the most fearsome centers in league history.

Because of his newfound focus on defense, Wilt Chamberlain was able to help the Lakers win 33 consecutive games from November 5, 1971, all the way to January 7, 1972. No other team in league history has ever been able to break that single season 33-game winning streak though the 2015-16 Golden State Warriors did so in a span of two seasons.

Wilt Chamberlain would end the season averaging a then all-time career low of 14.8 points together with a league-leading 19.2 rebounds. He also led the league in field goal percentage by making 65% of his shots. And because of Wilt unselfishness and focus on defense, the Lakers won 69 games, breaking the 68-win mark that the Big Dipper himself help set when he was still in Philadelphia.

The Lakers would sweep the Chicago Bulls in the first round to secure another meeting with the Milwaukee Bucks in the Conference Finals. While Kareem Abdul-Jabbar was still the league's MVP and the era's best player, Wilt Chamberlain was more focused and intent on getting back at the younger player that had been hogging the limelight away from him.

In what was considered the greatest matchup in basketball history, Wilt Chamberlain put up one of his most inspired playoff performances. Despite playing against a player 11 years his junior, Chamberlain defended Abdul-Jabbar well. And in Game 6 when the Lakers clinched the series win, the older Wilt the Stilt was running past Kareem during fastbreak opportunities. What Wilt did that series even made well-known writers say that he outplayed Kareem in that series.[ix]

Playing against a smaller Jerry Lucas in the NBA Finals when the Lakers met the Knicks once again, Wilt Chamberlain took over. The Knicks would nevertheless take Game 1, but injuries to key players would help the Lakers' cause. The Big Dipper would power the Los Angeles Lakers to four straight wins averaging 21.3 points and 24.3 rebounds in all those four games. This eventually led to a Laker win in five games.

With the way he played during the regular season and with his inspired performances during the playoffs, Wilt Chamberlain was a champion for the second time in his career. He would also be heralded as one of the players that brought a championship to Los Angeles for the first time since the team relocated from Minneapolis. And with that, Wilt was also able to solidify himself as one of the greatest players not only in Laker history but also in the history of the sport itself.

Final Season and Retirement

During the 1972-73 season, the Los Angeles Lakers were still one of the best teams in the league, but would fall short of expectations because of injuries to key players such as Jerry West and Happy Hairston. With Wilt focused more on defense and rebounding, the Lakers would be hard-pressed to find offense but would still win 60 games that season.

The 36-year old Wilt Chamberlain averaged 13.2 points, 18.6 rebounds, and 4.5 assists. He won his 11th title that season to secure his name as the league's all-time best rebounder. He would also shot a record of 72.7% from the floor and made sure that everything he attempted were efficient shots. No player has yet to break that record.

During the playoffs, the Lakers met with the Bulls once again, but had to beat them in seven games because of a hobbled Jerry West and an injured Happy Hairston. Wilt was extra active on the boards during that series as he averaged 24.6 rebounds against the Bulls in seven games. He performed just as well in the series against the newly relocated Golden State Warriors. He averaged 23.6 rebounds against his old team as his Lakers went on to win the series in five games.

Facing the New York Knicks in the Finals once again, the Los Angeles Lakers were just too injured and gassed to keep up with a healthy Knicks team. After winning Game 1, the Lakers would fall in the next four games due in large part to the fact that their stars were either too old or were injured. The final play that Wilt Chamberlain had in Game 5 was a dunk. Unknown to everyone and even himself, that was the last play he would ever have in the NBA.

True to his word back in the 60's, Wilt Chamberlain made his way to the ABA where he was hired by the San Diego Conquistadors for a hefty sum of $600,000 as a player coach. However, he was barred by legal action to play for San Diego because he still had a one-year option left on his contract with the Lakers. For most of that season, Wilt was absent as a coach for the Conquistadors as he felt bored that he was unable to play the game. He would eventually retire from basketball after that single season with the ABA.[viii]

Wilt Chamberlain retired from the game of basketball as then the only player to crack 30,000 career points and as the top scorer in league history. He totaled 31,419 career points and averaged 30.1 points over the course of his career. To this day, he still leads the league in career points per game average while sharing that record with Michael Jordan. He also retired with an NBA all-time high of 23,924 rebounds. No player has ever come close to that mark. Only he and Bill Russell have ever broken the 20,000-rebound barrier.

Despite all the scoring and rebounding achievements he had, what Wilt Chamberlain was probably most proud of was the fact that he was a two-time NBA champion. That was a title that often eluded him despite the fact that he was the all-time best player during his playing days and was often considered the most dominant man in all of basketball history. Nevertheless, what was important was that he retired as a champion and had no regrets about leaving basketball where he was putting up record after record. And in 1978, he was immediately selected to headline the class that would be enshrined forever in the Naismith Basketball Hall of Fame in Springfield, Massachusetts.

Chapter 6: Personal Life

The Biggest Star

Wilt Chamberlain was arguably basketball's biggest star during his playing years. No other player could command the large sum of money he was earning with all the teams he was playing for. He was a megastar not only as a basketball player but as a celebrity as well. Chamberlain was a major endorser for several brands and appeared in movies as well. There were even hints that he would fight boxing great Muhammad Ali, but such a spectacle never came to fruition.

As the biggest star in sports at that time, Wilt Chamberlain was an insomniac that loved the big city night life and the partying that came with it. Throughout his career in Philadelphia, he would even stay in New York to enjoy the night life. This was also considered one of the reasons why he requested to be in Los Angeles. The Big Dipper was particularly notorious as a man that loved the attention that women gave him. He is arguably basketball's all-time biggest playboy and often organized parties in his mansion. He loved partying and going out with women so much that he remained single and lived a solitary lifestyle until the time of his death in 1999.

Rivalries

One of the biggest parts of Wilt Chamberlain's personal life as an NBA player were the rivalries that came with it. With so much attention on him and with people constantly scrutinizing him, it could never be avoided that Chamberlain would have heated battles with a player or two during his life as a basketball player.

The most known rivalry that Wilt Chamberlain ever had was with the Boston Celtics' all-time great Bill Russell. What made that rivalry special aside from all the battles between the 60's two best centers was the fact that they had contrasting styles. Wilt came into the NBA as a dominant scorer that demanded the ball every possession. He would put up 50, 60, or even 70 points for his team. On the other hand, Bill Russell was a defensive specialist that took minimal shots. He was the consummate leader that thrived in making his teammates look good on the offensive end while making sure he was doing his job as a defender and rebounder at the opposite end of the floor.

Throughout their countless battles, Wilt Chamberlain would often fall short of beating Bill Russell, especially during the playoffs. However, on the individual level, there can be no argument that Wilt was always the better one-on-one player. Though Russell was often described as the best post defender in league history, not even he could stop Chamberlain. The best he could do was contain the dominant center.

Everything that Wilt and Bill had to go through in their battles with one another and every playoff game and Finals bout they had all contributed to the belief that their rivalry is perhaps the greatest in basketball history. While Larry Bird and Magic Johnson would later become fierce rivals in the 80's, the two players played different positions and would rarely match up with one another. On the other hand, Chamberlain and Russell were two giants that guarded each other every night they played. They relished in the prospect of getting physically intense with one another in their many on-court battles. Their rivalry made the stuff of legends. It was like Godzilla taking on King Kong.

On the team aspect, Bill Russell was the more accomplished of the two. He would win 11 NBA titles, and his five MVP awards were more of team accomplishments than they were individual accolades. On the other end, Wilt Chamberlain would win only two championships, but was named to the All-NBA First Team seven times and was an MVP four times.

Despite the fact that they were rivals on the basketball court, they were good friends outside the realm of the sport. Both players respected one another, though things became cold when Russell criticized Wilt after the 1969 NBA Finals. Their friendship would rekindle during the 80's when they resumed communication with one another. And when Wilt died in 1999, Bill was the second person to be notified of it.

Other than Bill Russell, Wilt Chamberlain also had a rivalry with the former Lew Alcindor, who is now Kareem Abdul-Jabbar. The two first met back in the middle of the 60's at a basketball tournament in New York when Abdul-Jabbar was still 17 years old. Wilt was impressed by the lanky seven-footer, and he immediately placed him within his inner circle. However, the relationship faded because of the battles the moment Kareem made it to the NBA.

When Kareem was drafted into the NBA, Wilt was already past his prime. Despite that, they still had plenty of playoff battles that contributed to the growing legends of both Chamberlain and Abdul-Jabbar. Had the two met when they were in the prime of their respective careers, their battles would have been more intense and legendary. Nevertheless, it was also a passing of the torch from one all-time great center to the next one. Kareem would become basketball's standard bearer long after Wilt retired and would also be the one to break Chamberlain's all-time career scoring record.

Death

Later on in his life, Wilt Chamberlain began to suffer irregularities in his heartbeat. It started in 1992 when he was hospitalized because of his heart problems. He would soon start to take medication to help him keep with his medical condition but would nevertheless deteriorate because of it. In 1999, his health declined so rapidly that, on October 12 of the same year, he passed away at the age of 63 because of congestive heart failure.

Chapter 7: Impact on Basketball

Probably the biggest impact Wilt Chamberlain has ever had on the game of basketball is his dominance as a player. While critics would often take away the fact that he was arguably the league's most dominant player because of the reason that he was playing in an era when players were smaller and much less athletic, size and athleticism were not the main reasons why the Big Dipper was unstoppable back then.

Standing 7'1" and weighing close to 300 pounds during his later years, Wilt Chamberlain was indeed a mountain of a man compared to players that stood nearly half a foot shorter than he was back then. Not only was he far bigger than any player back then but he was also far more superior as an athlete. He could jump higher than any player in the league, could run just as quick as a guard, and was as powerful as a professional bodybuilder. With that kind of a physical profile, it was not difficult to imagine how such a player could not dominate against 6'9" centers.

However, Wilt Chamberlain was not all about size and muscle. He arguably had the best stamina out of all the players that have ever played in the history of the league. He spent much of his career playing all 48 minutes of the games he played, and during the 1961-62 season, he even averaged more than 48 minutes a night. On top of it all, he had a vast arsenal of post moves. He thrived at driving from the low post, sealing off defenders, hitting hook shots and fadeaways, and making graceful finger rolls near the basket. Wilt was anything but an athlete that relied solely on his superior physical capabilities.

Because of how dominant Wilt Chamberlain was, several rule changes had to be implemented to make sure that no other player in the future would enjoy the advantages he had. The lane was widened so that he would be prevented from staying close to the basket because of the three-second rule. Offensive goaltending was also implemented to prevent Wilt from taking advantage of his teammates' shots to convert as his own, even though there was not an assurance of whether they would miss. And knowing how bad a foul shooter he was, Wilt would even use his 50-inch vertical leap to convert his free throws by dunking it from the foul line without a running start. The NBA would ban this kind of a tactic and would force the Big Dipper to shoot the ball from the free throw line.

As the most dominant player of his time, Wilt Chamberlain was also responsible for making superstar basketball players into megastar celebrities. No other player during his era commanded the same attention and star power he was getting. Basketball became much more popular because of him, and such a reputation as a superstar celebrity paved the way for future NBA players to get the same kind of star treatment as he did in the past.

Looking back at Wilt's career, nothing short of being dominant was his significant impact on the game of basketball. Whether it was on the court or off it, Wilt Chamberlain was a dominant figure in cage wars and news headlines. It did not matter where he played, what team he played for, and how he was playing. No matter what he did, he was literally and figuratively dominant simply because that was his nature. And when it comes right down to it, no other figure in NBA history may ever surpass Wilt Chamberlain's dominance.

Chapter 8: Legacy

Whether they may last or not, one of the best legacies that Wilt Chamberlain has left to the game of basketball was the records he put up during his career. Wilt holds the most number of records in league history, and he did so in all facets of the game. No other player has ever come close to equalling the number of records he has put up.

In scoring, Chamberlain holds the record for most points per game in a single season after tallying 50.4 points per game in 1962. He also holds the record for most points scored in a single season by going for 4,029 points the same year. And nobody could ever forget the 100 points he scored during the same year against the New York Knicks. To this date, Kobe Bryant's 81 points back in 2006 come closest to the record that Wilt has held for more than five decades.

And when Wilt Chamberlain retired, he held the record for all-time points scored in a career. He would soon be surpassed by only four other players in that regard. The first was Kareem Abdul-Jabbar, and Michael Jordan and Karl Malone soon followed. Kobe Bryant would later overtake him by more than 2,000 career points. However, Wilt still holds the record for career points per game average. With 30.1 points per game during his career, he shares the record with Michael Jordan.

Concerning rebounding, Wilt Chamberlain is also regarded as the league's all-time best rebounder. He led the league in rebounding 11 times and his 27.2 rebounds per game average back in 1961 is an

NBA record. He holds a career rebounding average of 22.9 while his 23,924 career rebounds seem to be an unbreakable mark. What is even more unbreakable was his 55-rebound game back in 1960. Today, not even an entire team could grab 55 rebounds a night.

Wilt Chamberlain is also considered to be one of the most versatile players in league history. He holds the record for most double-doubles of all time while also holding the record for the highest player efficiency rating of all time. His nine consecutive triple-doubles are also an NBA record. And on top of it all, the fact that he is the only center or big man to have ever led the league in assists is something that no other versatile player close to his size has ever come close to achieving.

While records would always be what would best define Wilt Chamberlain's legacy, one of the other legacies he has left to the NBA is the fact that he paved the way for similarly big and athletic centers to dominate the game as well. While Kareem Abdul-Jabbar may have succeeded him as the league's best player back in the 70's, several other athletic seven-footers found their way to become dominant figures in the league.

David Robinson dominated during the 90's, which is regarded as the Golden Age of centers, using his superior length, mobility, and athleticism. He would become a two-time NBA champion, an MVP, and a scoring leader in the process. Later = during the late 2000's and the early parts of the next decade, Dwight Howard used his athletic skills, strength, and quickness to dominate bigger but less physically gifted centers. While he was shorter than Wilt, his style and muscular build were closer to the Big Dipper than any other player in league history, though Howard would not come close to the latter's dominance.

No other player in league history has ever come closer to becoming mentioned in the same breath of Wilt Chamberlain's dominance than Shaquille O'Neal has. O'Neal, the biggest player in league history at 7'1" and 350 pounds, has the same kind of physical superiority that Chamberlain enjoyed throughout his career. Like Wilt, he was athletic and skilled down at the low post. Shaq was so dominant that he would command triple-teams and would also institute several rule changes during his prime as the league's most imposing player.

During the height of O'Neal's dominance, some would even say that he would have been more dominant than Wilt Chamberlain was if they had played in the same era. A mammoth of a man like Shaq would have bulldozed his way through the smaller players that Wilt played up against back in 60's. Although Shaquille O'Neal may be just as physically imposing and skilled as Wilt Chamberlain was, the one thing that the Big Dipper had over him was stamina. O'Neal's era may have bigger and more skilled and athletic players, but the pace and physicality were not the same as in Chamberlain's era. The fact that Wilt was playing all 48 minutes of a game during his prime means that he could have also done the same in any other era of basketball. But taking nothing away from O'Neal, Wilt Chamberlain paved the way for him to be just as dominant of a center as the Big Dipper was. He is arguably the only player in league history worthy to be compared to Wilt the Stilt.

In today's NBA, the giant center has nearly become extinct. Seven-footers have been dwelling outside the paint and even all the way out to the three-point line more often than they ever did. Only players such as Andre Drummond and DeAndre Jordan could come close to Wilt's profile as a player because of how they use their athleticism and size to their advantage.

While some would argue that Wilt would not thrive in today's NBA because of how much the game has evolved, the fact that Drummond and Jordan have become productive players for playoff contenders prove that Chamberlain would become just as great. Imagine a player with the same skills, stamina, and physical gifts as Wilt the Stilt manning the paint while three-point shooters roam free out on the perimeter. It only goes to prove that Wilt is not just a product of the times, but he is an all-time great talent no matter what era you put him in.

With all the records he shattered and still holds to this day, and taking into account how much he changed the game and paved the way for future generations to thrive in the NBA, one would only wonder if Wilt Chamberlain is a once-in-a-lifetime kind of a player that may never come again. He was an extraordinary athlete that captivated the imagination of basketball fans when the sport was still growing. Even today, people still talk about him like he was a mythological figure in the history of the NBA. But whether his accolades and records may be myths or not, what is certain is that numbers do not lie. And no matter how you look at it, the numbers are on the side of Wilt Chamberlain as the same numbers are primarily the reason as to why he is an immortal figure in basketball's Hall of Fame.

Final Word/About the Author

I was born and raised in Norwalk, Connecticut. Growing up, I could often be found spending many nights watching basketball, soccer, and football matches with my father in the family living room. I love sports and everything that sports can embody. I believe that sports are one of most genuine forms of competition, heart, and determination. I write my works to learn more about influential athletes in the hopes that from my writing, you the reader can walk away inspired to put in an equal if not greater amount of hard work and perseverance to pursue your goals. If you enjoyed *Wilt Chamberlain: The Inspiring Story of One of Basketball's Greatest Players*, please leave a review! Also, you can read more of my works on *Roger Federer, Novak Djokovic, Andrew Luck, Rob Gronkowski, Brett Favre, Calvin Johnson, Drew Brees, J.J. Watt, Colin Kaepernick, Aaron Rodgers, Peyton Manning, Tom Brady, Russell Wilson, Michael Jordan, LeBron James, Kyrie Irving, Klay Thompson, Stephen Curry, Kevin Durant, Russell Westbrook, Anthony Davis, Chris Paul, Blake Griffin, Kobe Bryant, Joakim Noah, Scottie Pippen, Carmelo Anthony, Kevin Love, Grant Hill, Tracy McGrady, Vince Carter, Patrick Ewing, Karl Malone, Tony Parker, Allen Iverson, Hakeem Olajuwon, Reggie Miller, Michael Carter-Williams, John Wall, James Harden, Tim Duncan, Steve Nash, Draymond Green, Kawhi Leonard, Dwyane Wade, Ray Allen, Pau Gasol, Dirk Nowitzki, Jimmy Butler, Paul Pierce, Manu Ginobili, Pete Maravich, Larry Bird, Kyle Lowry, Jason Kidd, David Robinson, LaMarcus Aldridge, Derrick Rose, Paul*

George, Kevin Garnett, Chris Paul, Marc Gasol, Yao Ming, Al Horford, Amar'e Stoudemire, DeMar DeRozan, Isaiah Thomas, Kemba Walker and Chris Bosh in the Kindle Store. If you love basketball, check out my website at claytongeoffreys.com to join my exclusive list where I let you know about my latest books and give you lots of goodies.

Like what you read? Please leave a review!

I write because I love sharing the stories of influential athletes like Wilt Chamberlain with fantastic readers like you. My readers inspire me to write more so please do not hesitate to let me know what you thought by leaving a review! If you love books on life, basketball, or productivity, check out my website at claytongeoffreys.com to join my exclusive list where I let you know about my latest books. Aside from being the first to hear about my latest releases, you can also download a free copy of *33 Life Lessons: Success Principles, Career Advice & Habits of Successful People*. See you there!

Clayton

References

[i] JT, Richard. "Wilt Chamberlain: Did He Really Play In a Weak Era?". *Bleacher Report.* 19 August 2010. Web.

[ii] Bock, Hal. "More Than a Big Man, Wilt Was a Giant". *ESPN.* 13 October 1999. Web.

[iii] Wessler, Kirk. "B.H. 'Bert' Born, Kansas and Peoria basketball star, dies at 80". *Journal Star.* 4 February 2013. Web.

[iv] Pierce, Dan. "Chamberlain Rated Greatest in Court Game". *Sporting News.* 21 December 1955. Web.

[v] *NBA.com.* Web

[vi] Smith, Steve. "Greatness Revisited: Why Wilt Chamberlain Was the Greatest NBA Player Ever". *Bleacher Report.* 27 February 2009. Web.

[vii] "Wilt Scores 100!". *NBA.com.* Web.

[viii] Cherry, Robert (2004). *Wilt: larger than life.* Chicago, Illinois. Triumph Books.

[ix] "One for the Dipper". *Time.* 22 May 1972. Web.